FOOTBALL 101

Brenda,
Best wishes
George
Darlington

FOOTBALL 101

By University of Nebraska Assistant Coach

GEORGE DARLINGTON

with Bob Schaller

Illustrated by Paul Fell

CROSSTRAINING PUBLISHING

Football 101

Football 101, George Darlington

ISBN 1-887002-86-3

Cross Training Publishing
317 West Second Street
Grand Island, NE 68801
(308) 384-5762

This book is manufactured in the United States of America.

Library of Congress Cataloging in Publication Data in Progress.

Published by Cross Training Publishing
317 West Second Street
Grand Island, NE 68801
1-800-430-8588
Publisher website: www.crosstrainingpub.com

FOREWORD

For the past two decades, I have had the pleasure of teaching a course entitled "Football Facts for Novices." What began originally as a course exclusively for women has evolved into a coed offering. Over time it apparently became socially acceptable, at least in Lincoln, Nebraska, for arm-chair quarterbacks to admit that they don't know as much about the game as they thought.

During six two-hour sessions, the students watch video tapes, walk and jog through football maneuvers, as well as refer to their playbooks and NCAA "Read-Easy Football Rules." Numerous questions are also answered to increase the students' knowledge of the great game of "American football."

At the urging of many students, I have produced this book to aid you in increasing your understanding and knowledge of the various aspects of the sport of football. In addition, this increased knowledge will allow you, while attending games or watching on TV, to follow the action and "be in the know."

Football is not a science in a technical sense, yet it is in a practical sense. Strengths and weaknesses are dissected and evaluated by teams daily.

Football is more than a hobby to those who play and coach the game.

If you have just been introduced to the game or are learning because someone close to you is a football aficionado, this book should help push you far beyond intro status. You might enter this book a beginner when it comes to football knowledge. However, by the time you get through with it, you should know the game well enough to not only carry on dialogue while watching it, but understand what is unfolding before you.

We will start with a look at the make-up of the game, an introduction to the different positions and players. A comment many non-fans make is, "Boy, that guy looks too small to be a football player." Yet there are dozens of players in the NFL who weigh 180 pounds or less. At the same time, the game is still one of strength, along with speed. To that end, the 300-pound player is more common than ever before in the history of the game.

Hopefully you will be entertained as well as educated as you work through the material. In addition you can refer to the material as different situations arise in viewing future games.

CONTENTS

CHAPTER 1

A Game of Brains, Not Simply Brawn

Football is a game that includes players of different shapes, sizes and temperaments. These differences are what make a team unique. To have all the same kind of players would be horrible.

The differences and how bonds are developed and strengthened are what give teams chemistry as well as personality.

Football 101 is a road map. But there is more than one entry point in this book. Beginners will see how football is not just a bunch of big bodies ramming into each other. The sport is far more cerebral than it is physical. Although the physical aspect is crucial because all teams have big, strong, fast players, it is the ability to perform as a team and execute better than an opponent that makes one team a winner.

Players and fans who know a little about the game will learn more in the pages that follow. There is something, I believe, even for the most advanced fan.

Television programs such as ESPN's *NFL Primetime* and Fox Sports' *Hardcore Football* have brought attention to plays and formations by drawing them up and showing them in action. There is so much going on during a game that is prepared off the field, before the snap of the ball.

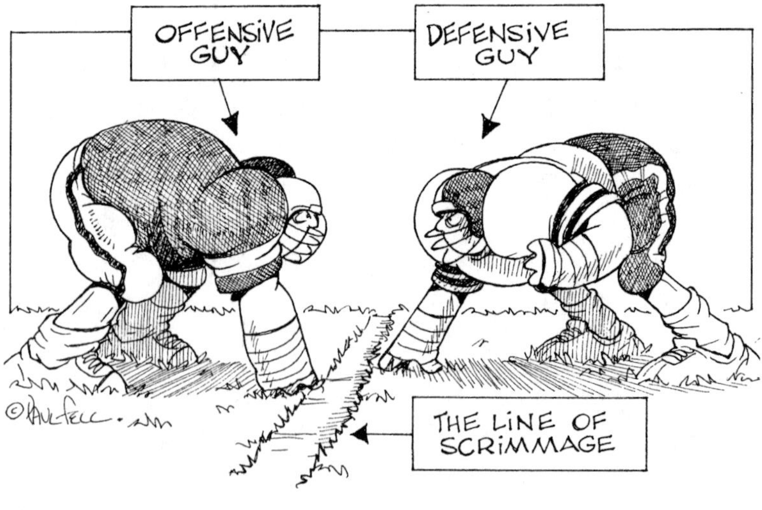

In fact, when teams are at the line of scrimmage, the play has already, in effect, begun. The defense will scramble to adjust as the offense reveals its formation. The defense will further adjust if a player goes "in motion" before the ball is snapped.

Conversely, the offense will have to adapt as defensive linemen move around on the line of scrimmage, seeking the quickest possible route into the backfield. The blocking assignments for the offensive line and fullback can change several times in the few seconds that the teams are lined up as the quarterback calls out signals. Those signals might also change if the quarterback recognizes a different coverage plan than the defense is planning to use. If the defense brings more players to the line of scrimmage, the quarterback will have to notice—or "read"—that and change the play if the situation warrants it.

If the play the offense is going to run is designed to go inside, there is no use in keeping that play if eight or nine defenders are clogging the line of scrimmage. The quarterback might change the play to a running play to the outside or a fake handoff and pass, since there are not many defenders left to cover the outside receivers.

It must be recognized that football is a game of chess as much as it is a game of muscle.

Sitting in ROTC class midway through the first semester of my freshman year at Rutgers in 1957, I learned that the portable classroom was on the same field where the first college football game had been played decades earlier. During that inaugural contest, Rutgers defeated Princeton.

The game of football has changed considerably since that first game between Rutgers and Princeton. Interest in the game has reached astronomical heights that could never have been envisioned, even by the biggest football fanatics from the early days. With the advent of the domed stadium, football is even played indoors. I wonder if anyone present during the origin of football ever imagined the game being played inside.

And there are now all kinds of football: at the high school level, there is 6-man, 8-man and the traditional 11-man football (which is the case in college and the NFL). There is the Canadian Football League, which uses 12 players on the field for each team and plays on a wider and longer field.

Yet the game of American football has remained basically the same in many ways. The goal is still to get the ball in the end zone. And the game is, despite the marketing trends and the high-profile superstars, still very much a team sport. Teams will not win unless every player makes a big contribution. While there is much more of an emphasis on passing—or throwing—the ball than ever before, teams know they must have success running the ball first. This allows them a better opportunity to pass on a defense that expects the team to run.

The purpose of this book is to aid all fans in their enjoyment of the game. And remember: follow the ball when you can. We will give you tips on how to do that as well.

CHAPTER 2

The Players

Offense (diagram 2-1)

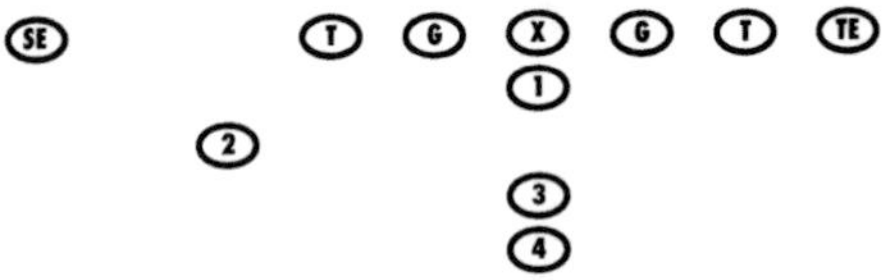

2-1 Backfield Numbering System

Quarterback: Lines up behind the center, either directly or back about six yards (shot-gun formation). The quarterback hands the ball off, or pitches it, to the running back or fullback, runs the ball himself or passes the ball. He must also designate when the ball is to be snapped. When he approaches the line of scrimmage and the players line up, the quarterback is responsible for recognizing the defensive formation to see if he should "audible" (change the play).

Ideal specifications: 6-feet to 6-4, 200 pounds to about 225. Must be mobile and relatively quick, if not fast (speed is a bonus, and lateral speed is essential for a quarterback in a running offense). However, the most important thing for a quarterback to possess is an ability to move the team and score touchdowns. Therefore, he must understand the offense and be able to understand and communicate clearly with the coach and the other offensive players.

Running back: Lines up in the offensive backfield. Takes a handoff or pitch from the quarterback. Also might go out for a pass or help block on a passing play.

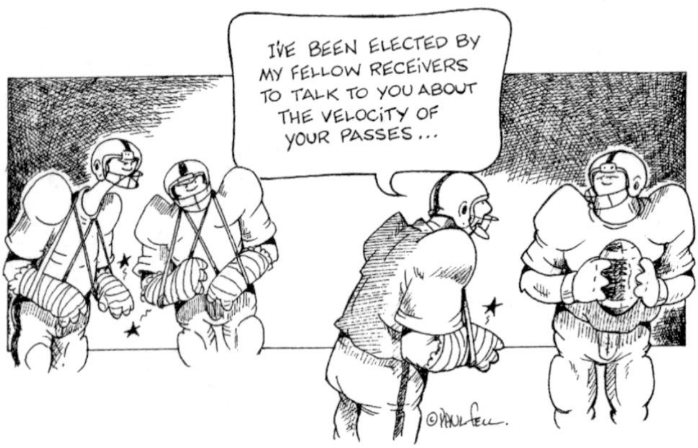

Ideal specifications: 5-feet-9 to 6-2, 190 pounds or larger. Needs a time of 4.6 seconds or faster in the 40-yard dash.

Fullback: Lines up in the offensive backfield, directly behind the quarterback in the I-formation or parallel to the running back in a tandem-back set. Takes a handoff from the quarterback on running plays. Blocks for the running back on running plays. Either stays in to block or goes out for a pass on passing plays.

Ideal specifications: 5-feet-10 to 6-1, 210 pounds or larger with a time of 4.7 seconds or faster in the 40-yard dash.

Tight end: Lines up on either end of the line of scrimmage next to an offensive tackle. Blocks on running plays, usually a receiver on passing plays.

Ideal specifications: 6-feet-3 or taller, 235 pounds minimum, maxing out at 255-260 if speed is maintained, a time of 4.8 seconds or faster in the 40-yard dash.

Offensive tackles (two, left and right): Line up next to offensive guards on line of scrimmage, block on passing and running plays.

Ideal specifications: 6-feet-4 to 6-7, minimum of 280 pounds (most at the major colleges and professional level are at least 300 pounds), a time of 5.1 seconds or faster in the 40-yard dash.

Offensive guards (two, left and right): Line up on either side of center at line of scrimmage. Block on running and passing plays. Called upon to pull on trap plays and other running plays and during screen passes. Note: The guards are very important to the fan in terms of following the ball. This will be discussed in more detail later.

Ideal specifications: 6-feet-2 or taller, 280 pounds or larger and a time of 5.0 seconds or faster in the 40-yard dash.

Center: Lines up on line of scrimmage, snaps the ball and is responsible for making "line calls" when he recognizes the defensive scheme. Usually blocks a defensive tackle or nose guard, or picks up a blitzing player at times, as do other linemen.

Ideal specifications: 6-feet-1 to 6-4, 280 pounds or larger, with a time of 5.0 seconds or faster in the 40-yard dash.

Wide receivers (usually two, also called split end or flanker, depending on set): Line up either on or off the line of scrimmage, far away from the offensive line, although they are sometimes in a "slot," usually on passing downs. Called upon to block on running plays and as receivers on passing plays.

Ideal specifications: 5-feet-9 or taller (the trend in the NFL is toward taller, bigger wide receivers, since they are usually covered by smaller, lighter cornerbacks), 180-210 pounds, no slower than 4.5 or 4.6 seconds in the 40-yard dash.

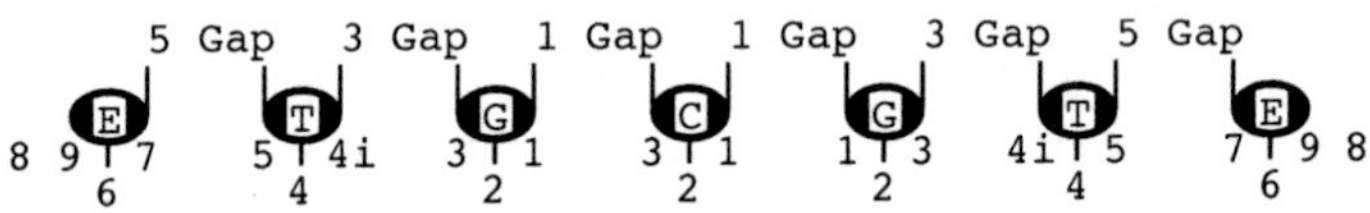

0 Technique - Head up to Center
2 Technique - Head up to Guard
4 Technique - Head up to Tackle
6 Technique - Head up to End
8 Technique - True End
1 Technique - Inside shoulder of Guard
3 Technique - Outside shoulder of Guard
4i Technique - Inside shoulder of Tackle
5 Technique - Outside shoulder of Tackle
7 Technique - Inside shoulder of End or WB
9 Technique - Outside shoulder of End or WB
1 Gap Technique - Equal distance betweenCenter and Guard
3 Gap Technique - Equal distance betweenGuard and Tackle
5 Gap Technique - Equal distance betweenTackle and End

2-2 Defensive Front Alignments

Defensive tackles two, (note, in 3-4 defensive formation there is only one, and he is called a "nose guard"): Line up on the line of scrimmage to seal gaps in the guards—center area— is the key to stopping the run, and generating inside pressure on passing plays.

Ideal specifications: 6-feet-3 to 6-5, 275 pounds to 300-plus in some cases, a time of 4.8 seconds or faster in the 40-yard dash.

Defensive ends (two): Line up outside the offensive tackles on the line of scrimmage. Called on to contain outside offensive tackles. In most cases responsible for rushing the passer from outside–in on passing plays.

Ideal specifications: Depending on whether the outside defensive lineman is used as a "rush end" (like at Nebraska) or in a 3-4 defense, the size varies. Generally, the defensive ends are 6-feet-3 to 6-5, 260 to 285 pounds, with a time of 4.8 seconds or faster in the 40-yard dash.

Outside linebackers (two, left and right, or weak-side and strong-side): Line up usually a couple of yards off of the line of scrimmage. Called on to force the run inside and make tackles on running plays. Sometimes called on to cover running backs and tight ends on passing plays or to rush the passer.

Ideal specifications: 6-feet-2 to 6-4, 225 to 240 pounds (depending on the defense scheme and formation), time of 4.7 seconds or faster in the 40-yard dash.

Inside linebackers (two, in 3-4 alignment, but only one middle linebacker in 4-3 formation: Often referred to as the "quarterbacks of the defense." Line up directly in front of the offensive line, usually two to five yards off the line of scrimmage. Identifies the offensive formation and switches defenses when necessary. Must be a good run-stopper and cover backs coming out of the backfield on passing plays, or even cover the tight end. Sometimes rushes the quarterback on passing plays rather than cover eligible receivers. Must often fight off blocking attempts by huge linemen to get to the ball carrier.

Ideal specifications: 6-feet-3 to 6-5, 235 to 260 pounds, with a time of 4.8 seconds or faster in the 40-yard dash.

Cornerbacks (two, left and right): Line up outside on the offense's wide receivers. Must be quick and be able to "cover" (run alongside) receivers. Must fight off receiver's blocks on running plays.

Ideal specifications: 5-feet-10 or taller, 180 pounds to 210 (depending on height), a time of 4.5 seconds in the 40-yard dash.

Safeties (two, position names vary): Line up between the cornerbacks in the secondary, or near the line of scrimmage when they are covering a tight end or back coming out of the backfield. While the defensive backs' main responsibility is to stop the pass, they also may be key to stopping running plays. Normally, the larger safeties are called upon more often to make key tackles on running plays.

Ideal specifications: 6-feet to 6-2, 200 pounds to 225, a time of 4.6 seconds in the 40-yard dash.

For a football team to be successful, it must combine a diverse collection of individual athletes into a smoothly operating unit. Each position on the field requires a distinct set of physical, mental and even emotional attributes. The offensive team is made up of skilled positions and linemen. The key skill position is the quarterback. The successes of teams are tied in large part to the performance of their quarterbacks. Running backs and receivers complete the skill position lineup. Of course, all players, regardless of position, must have certain skills. A lineman's skills are different than others but are of equal importance. Often the only time offensive line play is noticed is when an error is made. When a lineman jumps offside or allows a defensive player to get past him to tackle a teammate, he draws attention.

In the last 26 years there has been a startling change in the size of players. The following page shows a chart that compares the offensive and defensive tackles, ends, and linebackers reveals the stark physical change between the 1971 University of Nebraska football team and the 1997 Huskers. The players have gotten so much bigger that it is almost hard to believe. What will those sizes be in 20 years—400-pound linemen? It is certainly possible, especially if they can maintain or increase their speed at those sizes. Note the size differential—and keep in mind that the bigger players from today aren't just bigger—they are, in almost every case, faster than their lighter counterpart. Weightlifting and conditioning has, like car building and forms of medical science, made tremendous strides over the years. Thus, the players are now bigger, faster and stronger than ever before. It makes the game more exciting, but also more dangerous as these players collide at a frightening speed.

1971 HUSKERS

Offense Tackles
Marvin Crenshaw, 6-feet-5, 223
Carl Johnson, 6-feet-4, 252

Guards
Dick Rupert, 6-2, 221
Keith Wortman, 6-3, 238

Center
Bill Janssen, 6-3, 218

1971 offensive line total: 1,152

Defense Ends
Willie Harper, 6-3, 205
John Hyland, 6-2, 198

Tackles
Larry Jacobson, 6-6, 247
Dave Walline, 6-2, 238

Linebacker
Jerry Murtaugh, 6-3, 212

1971 defensive front five: 1,100

1997 HUSKERS

Offense Tackles
Eric Anderson, 6-4, 305—plus 82 pounds
Fred Pollack, 6-4, 305—plus 53

Guards
Aaron Taylor, 6-1, 305—plus 84
Jon Zatechka, 6-2, 290—plus 52

Center
Josh Heskew, 6-3, 280—plus 62

1997 offensive line total: 1,485—plus 333

Defense Ends
Grant Wistrom, 6-5, 255—plus 50
Mike Rucker, 6-6, 250—plus 52

Tackles
Jason Peter, 6-5, 285—plus 38
Jason Wiltz, 6-3, 310—plus 72

Linebacker
Jay Foreman, 6-1, 235—plus 23

1997 defensive front five: 1,335—plus 235

CHAPTER 3

A Bunch of Different "Guys"

The Big Guys

Offensive linemen—centers, guards and tackles—generally are the largest men on the team. The most successful offensive linemen are controlled, well-disciplined and cerebral. In fact, on many college teams, this group of players will have the highest grade point average.

Defensive linemen—tackles and ends, occasionally including a nose guard depending on the formation—may be nearly as large as the offensive linemen, but they generally are more aggressive, more animated and have a greater desire to do bodily harm. The defensive line is made up of two tackles and two ends.

The Little Guys

Wide receivers and defensive backs are smaller, quicker and faster than the linemen. They are called upon to perform many tasks completely foreign to the linemen. The wide receivers' positions vary greatly depending upon the offensive formation and strategy. They include split ends, wide outs and flankers. The defensive back group may also vary in number in a formation and nomenclature. They are made up of cornerbacks, nickel backs, strong safeties, and free or weak safeties.

Defensive backs have a lot of responsibilities. While they are often tackling players their size or smaller—wide receivers—they could just as easily find themselves pulling down a tight end who outweighs them by 50 pounds. Or they could find themselves being blocked by 300-plus pound offensive linemen on running plays.

Running backs can be of varied sizes but generally will fall in size somewhere between the tight ends and the wide receivers or defensive backs. This group can be broken down into two groups; those who are primarily blockers and those who are primarily runners. The former group is generally referred to as fullbacks, the latter as I-backs, halfbacks or running backs. A fullback will vary from a halfback in that he will be called upon to block more and carry the ball less, thus they are generally larger.

The Multi-Purpose Guys

The tight end position calls for players similar to both the wide receivers and offensive linemen in skills. Not as large as the offensive linemen, they are still called upon to be blockers for the running plays against big defensive linemen and linebackers. Also, they must be good receivers and avoid defenders to catch passes, even though they are much larger than wide receivers.

Linebackers should be larger than the defensive backs, smaller than the defensive linemen, but possess attributes of both. They are broken down into inside and outside linebacker positions. They must have quickness, agility and speed to pursue and tackle ball carriers and cover receivers, but also must be strong enough to shed the blocks of offensive linemen. They should be the most aggressive "wild and crazy guys" on the team.

The Main Man

A quarterback must possess skills and attributes that mesh with his coach's offensive philosophy. If the coach prefers to run option plays with "bootleg "and "play action" passes, he wants a fast and agile quarterback with a decent arm. The option quarterback may not be especially tall.

On the other hand, if the coach prefers to use his quarterback primarily as a drop-back passer, then he wants a taller player (one who can see over the rushing defensive linemen) with an accurate and powerful arm. The drop-back quarterback may not be as mobile as the option quarterback.

Regardless of a team's offensive style, the one attribute a quarterback must possess is the ability to move his team to score touchdowns. The most important six inches on the football field is between the quarterback's ears.

He must possess intelligence to understand the offense, perception to read the defense, and the ability to "automatic" (change or audible) to plays in response to the defense's alignments and adjustments.

Offensive linemen are called upon to block the defenders, to open holes for the running backs, and to pass protect against the defenders to allow the quarterback time to throw the ball. (In fact, unless the pass is tipped, they are not allowed to legally catch a pass). A lineman can pick up and run with a fumble or simply fall on it for a recovery.

Of the offensive linemen, the center snaps the ball between his legs to the quarterback. Normally the ball is handed directly to the quarterback, but sometimes it is passed several yards back to a quarterback in the "shot gun" alignment or on kicking plays to a holder (for a point after touchdown kick attempt, called a "PAT," and field-goal attempts) or to a punter. Obviously, it is important for the center not to be ticklish!

Tight ends must be good blockers as linemen but also be good receivers for passing situations.

Wide receivers must catch passes and have fine running skills, but also block on running plays. In fact, some are "called upon" but do very little about accomplishing their blocking chores.

The halfback or I-back (the main man, especially for a run-based offense like at Nebraska) must possess excellent running skills, explosiveness, elusiveness and speed to score touchdowns. Also, he must block for the fullback when he is running the ball. He and the fullback must block for the quarterback on passing plays or become a receiver as the play dictates.

The fullback is often a "glorified guard." A big, powerful, tough "blue collar" guy whose primary function is to block.

Defensive linemen must be able to defeat the tight end and offensive linemen's blocking attempts, rush to "sack" the quarterback or pursue to tackle the running back.

Defensive backs primarily must be able to cover receivers man-to-man or drop into areas (zones) versus passing plays. At times they must also "come up" to tackle running backs.

Of the defensive backs, the safeties normally are called upon to make more tackles, and the cornerbacks must cover the receiver more in man-to-man situations.

Linebackers must do it all. Primarily, they must tackle the running back, but also may be called upon to rush the passer on passing plays (blitz or "Red Dog") or drop to an area or even cover a receiver man-to-man.

The inside linebackers, usually the largest of the linebackers, spend more time defending the running game than the outside linebackers, who are usually faster.

The game of football has changed much in the last 50 years. Equipment has become much lighter and more protective.

The game is sometimes played on artificial turf or on "fancy" grass, also known as prescription turf (grass growing between nylon mesh).

Many rules have been altered, making the game much safer in many ways for the players. In addition, other rules have been changed to enhance the opportunity for more scoring, especially in the National Football League. Liberalizing "holding" by the offensive linemen and a limited ability for defensive backs to "jam" receivers past five yards from the line of scrimmage are two of the changes created to aid the offense. (note–This prohibition is only for the professional game).

CHAPTER 4

The Kickoff and What Follows

After a kickoff (the formation for both the kicking and receiving teams are shown in Diagram 4-1) a team takes over wherever its player was tackled, ran out of bounds, or where the ball went out of bounds. On a kickoff, however, the kicking team is penalized if the ball goes out of bounds, even if it bounces first. If the ball is kicked out of bounds, the receiving team gets the ball at that spot or at the 35-yard line, whichever is the most advantageous. Of course, it's better to kick the ball out of (over) the end zone because then the receiving team must take the ball at the 20-yard line.

Wherever a team takes over after receiving a kickoff or punt, they have four attempts called "downs" to progress ten yards to make a first "down," and 10 yards to go for another first down. Should the offense not achieve 10 yards on the first play, it would then be second down.

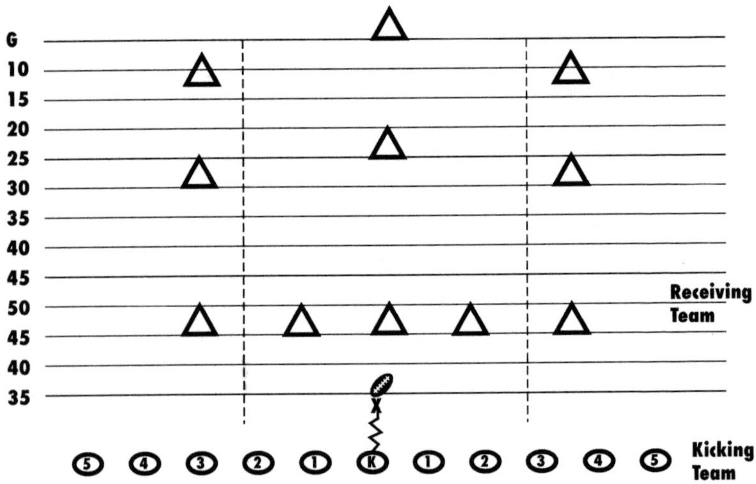

4-1 Formation for Both Kicking and Receiving on Kickoffs

For example, the offense gets four yards on first down on a running play or passing play; it would then be second down and six yards to go for a first down. On second down and six yards, they might pass and get six or more yards, which would result in a first down.

The 10 yards needed for a first down are from where the last first down is achieved—that is, if you have first down and 10 yards to go from your own 20, you must get at least to your own 30-yard line for the first down. But say you have a really good play and get to the 34-yard line, which is more than enough yards for the first down. The extra four yards picked up do not count against the upcoming first down and 10—it is now first down and 10 yards from the 34-yard line, meaning your team must get at least to the 44-yard line for its next first down.

But let's say on first down the offense runs the ball and gets five yards. That would make it second down and five yards to go for a first down. Then the team passes the ball, but the pass is incomplete (an incomplete pass results in no net yards). So that sets up third down and five. And then the offense runs the ball and gets only two yards. That would bring up fourth down and three yards.

If it is not late in the game during a very close contest, the offense usually punts on fourth down, especially if the offense needs more than one yard to get a first down. If a team is doing well and needs only a yard, they might go for it. If they get at least the one yard, then it is first down, and the sequence starts again. However, if on that play the offense fails to pick up the yard, the defensive team takes over at that exact spot. So if you are on your own 15-yard line and you fail on fourth down, the other team gets the ball and needs to go only 15 yards for a touchdown (or kick a field goal for three points from right there should they fail in moving the ball on first, second and third downs).

So teams are more prone to take the chance of "going for it" ("it" being the first down) on fourth down only when relatively deep in the other team's half of the field. Of course, if a team is trailing by, say, four points with only a minute left in the game, they will go for it on fourth down from just about anywhere on the field. While going for it on fourth down in your own half of the field is dangerous, giving the other team the ball while your team is trailing with only a minute left in the game seals the loss. Because if you don't have the ball, the other team will attempt running plays to run time off the clock. Unless the defensive team can force and recover a fumble, they will never get the ball back before the end of the game.

Back to the sequence of downs for a moment. If a team faces, say, fourth down and five yards, they will likely choose to punt. This is done because a punt allows the offensive team to have their punter kick the ball down the field, often 40 yards or so. If the offense is facing fourth down and five yards from its own 40-yard line, and it punts the ball 40 yards and the opposing team does not return it at all (say the ball bounces out of bounds—which is not a penalty on punts, only on kickoffs—or the return man is tackled immediately after catching it), that team would take over at its own 20-yard line, meaning they have to go 80 yards to score. Now, doesn't that sound better than failing to achieve fourth down and leaving the other team only 40 yards from a touchdown?

CHAPTER 5

The "Downs" and "Drives"

First down is a good time for a lot of teams to run the ball. Running the ball, as you will see later in the book, is important. If the ball is run successfully, the defense has to "key" on the run, and that makes the defense more susceptible to the pass. At Nebraska we often run on first down, especially to start a game. However, if we see on film that a defense has a tendency that would make them vulnerable to a pass on first down, we might try that.

FIRST DOWNS...
DEFENSE TRIES TO KEEP OPPONENT FROM ADVANCING BALL.
TEAM WITH BALL HAS 4 CHANCES TO MOVE AHEAD 10 YARDS.
10 YD
IF THE OFFENSE FAILS TO MAKE A FIRST DOWN ON ITS FOURTH ATTEMPT, DEFENSE TAKES POSSESSION OF THE BALL AT THAT POINT ON THE FIELD.
AFTER 3 UNSUCCESSFUL TRIES TO ADVANCE 10 YARDS, OFFENSE MUST DECIDE TO MAKE ONE MORE ATTEMPT OR TO PUNT, PUTTING THE DEFENSE DEEP IN ITS OWN TERRITORY.

First down is important because it sets the tone for that "drive" (each possession is called a drive). And if you fail to get more than two or three yards on first down, the chances are you might have to pass on second and third downs because you still need seven or eight yards for a new first down. Passing involves much more risk than running the ball. If, however, you attain six or seven yards on first down, you need a mere three or four yards for a first down.

That sets you up to where you can run it because you need only a few yards, or you can surprise them with a passing play and perhaps gain not just a first down, but maybe a whole bunch of yards—maybe even a touchdown.

If you are facing a long way to go for a first down on a second down play, most of the time you should attempt a passing play. But at the same time, you will still have another try (third down) if you don't pick up the remainder of the 10 yards you need for a first down.

Teams would much rather have third down and one or two, than third down and nine or 10 yards to go for a first down. If you are facing "third and long," your opponent knows you probably have to pass to pick up that many yards, and they can put in a defensive scheme geared toward stopping passing plays. If you have "third and short," you can either run the ball, or again surprise them with a fake run and throw the ball (called play-action pass, which is explored in more detail later). This could result in a larger gain of yardage.

Turnovers

Another key to understanding the game of football is the importance of turnovers.

A turnover is a fumble or interception that gives possession of the football to the opposing team. A fumble is most often recognized when an offensive player running with the ball—or a quarterback getting ready to pass or a receiver running with the ball after the catch—drops the ball or has it "stripped" (pulled out of his hands by a defensive player). A fumble can also happen on a punt or kickoff return. It also happens, less frequently, when a defensive player intercepts

OKAY, LAMONT... LET'S GO OVER THIS ONE MORE TIME. STRIP THE BALL FROM THE OPPONENT... GOT IT..?

(another form of turnover) a pass and then fumbles it while running it back.

Another kind of turnover is the interception. This occurs when the offense is passing. While there are halfback passes and passes made during a reverse by a receiver, the quarterback is the one throwing the ball more than 99 percent of the time. The interception occurs when the quarterback throws the ball, and it is caught by a member of the other team. There are several reasons for an interception:

1. A poor pass by the quarterback where he does not throw the ball to his receiver.

2. The receiver does not run to where the quarterback expects him to be, according to the play called. A defensive player may be the only one there, and thus comes up with the interception.

3. The quarterback throws the ball, and it is tipped or deflected by a member of either team. When the ball is tipped and sails up into the air or off course, it is basically a free ball.

4. A defensive player out-jumps a receiver on a well-thrown ball.

Fumbles and interceptions often change the momentum from one team to another. Players prone to turn the ball over see their playing time diminish. Often winning teams have a big positive turnover ratio (turnovers gained as opposed to turnovers lost).

Coaches stress the importance of "taking care of the ball." If you have the the ball, you must treat it as the most important possession you own.

©PAUL FELL

CHAPTER 6

Offense

The phase of football in which most people are interested is offense. The thrill of seeing a well-run play that allows a running back to make a significant gain or a well-thrown pass and a great catch can bring the fans to their feet.

Here is the one key for all fans—from novice to advanced, including scouts watching the game from the pressbox: watch the offensive guards if you want to follow the ball. The guards will block in the direction of the play. If the play is to the offensive team's right, the guards will attack in that direction, or one or both of them will lead the play that direction. At the same time, the quarterback will hand the ball off or even pitch it to a running back. The running back will head in the direction of the guards, who are busy moving defenders out of the way as they lead the play.

The guards retreat when the quarterback is going to pass the ball. The guards will also retreat on a "draw" play where the quarterback backs up as though he is going to pass, but then hands off as he finishes backpedaling. Even if the quarterback heads the opposite direction of the guards when he takes the snap, you should continue to follow the guards. Whoever the quarterback hands the ball to, or throws to on a screen pass, is bound to follow the guards more than 90 percent of the time.

The Running Game

Running plays will be developed to attack most of the gaps in the line, called holes. More than one play will often attack the same hole. Generally, there will be more plays directed at the one and nine holes as well as the two and eight holes. The holes are shown in Diagram 6-1.

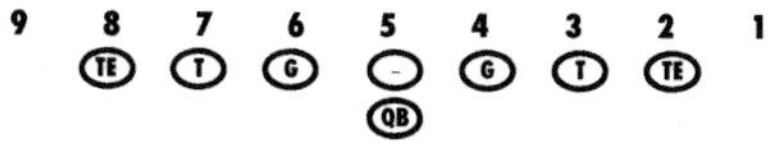

6-1 Hole Numbering System

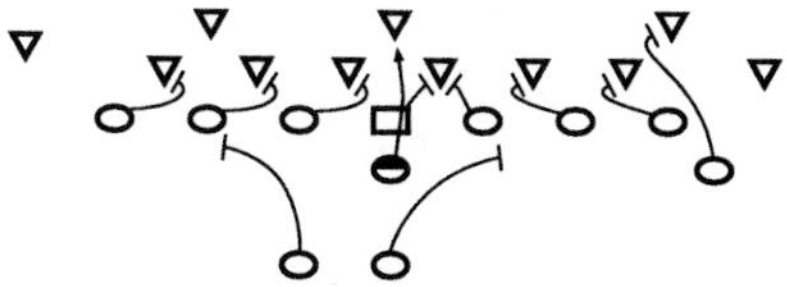

6-2 15 Smash

The simplest of all running plays is the quarterback sneak. The designation of the play would be "15 smash," Diagram 6-2. The quarterback would receive the ball and go straight ahead. The defensive alignment could force the quarterback to veer into the four or six hole.

This play is used in short-yardage situations. Third down and one yard or less, or fourth down and one yard or less are the typical situations. In addition, this play is often used inside the opponent's five-yard line. Sometimes the line wedge blocks. This is where the linemen attack toward one defender, thus double teaming a defender and cutting off other defensive players.

The play "44 isolation" involves the running back following the fullback toward the four hole, Diagram 6-3. The fullback blocks the isolated linebacker. The running back cuts off of the fullback's block. The lineman opens the hole for the backs to run. A double team on the nose guard is common. This play can be used on the goal line and in short-yardage situations. It can also be used in normal yardage situations.

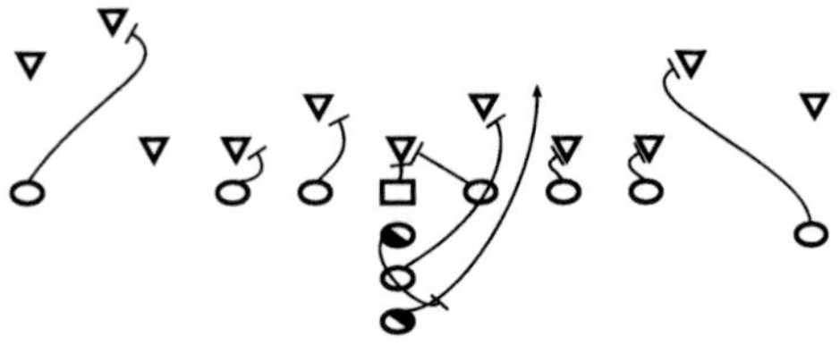

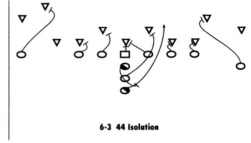

6-3 44 Isolation

To counteract aggressive defensive linemen, a trap play can be most effective, Diagram 6-4. The defensive lineman to be trapped is invited to charge. Then the trapper blocks the lineman from the side. The quarterback and I-backs continue faking to the outside to draw defenders with them while the fullback carries the football. This play is effective in any situation.

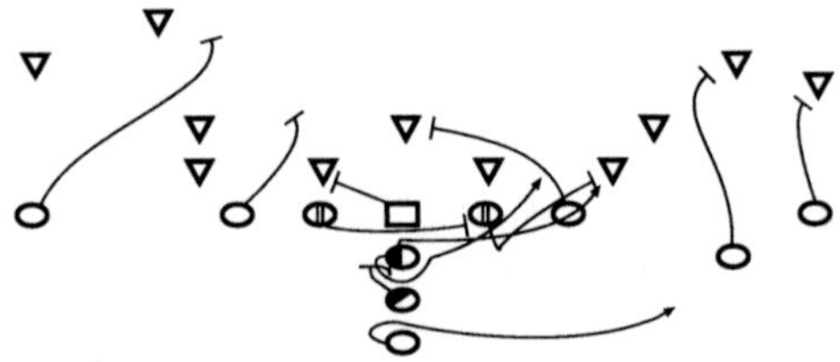

6-4 34 Trap

Another play that is very effective is a draw play, Diagram 6-5. The defensive linemen are invited to rush the quarterback who appears to be preparing to pass. Then the ball is slipped to a fullback while the blockers aggressively steer the defenders away from the hole.

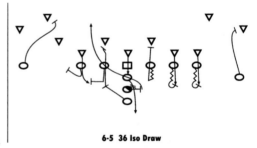

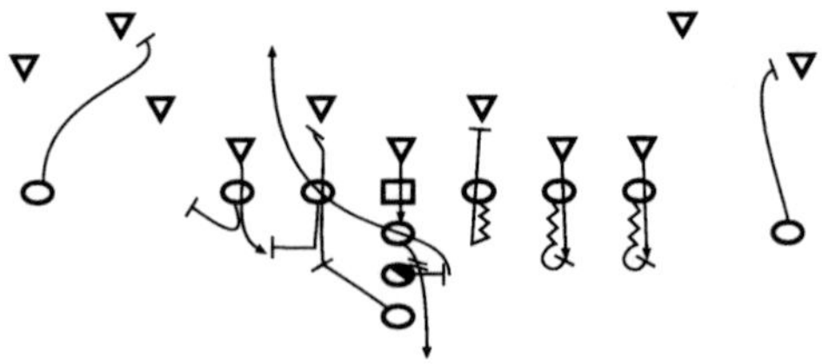

6-5 36 Iso Draw

A play dubbed "48G power" attacks the eight hole with a double team block, a kick out block and a guard leading through the hole, Diagram 6-6. There is no attempt at trickery. It is simply a tough, aggressive attack of the defense.

The most basic type of option play is the dive option. Some people refer to this play as a triple option. The first option is for the ball to be handed to the fullback. The second option is for the quarterback to keep the ball and run himself. The third option is for the ball to be pitched to the halfback (or I-back.) During the option play, the quarterback must correctly read the defense to determine which option to choose. Diagrams 6-7A, 6-7B and 6-7C.

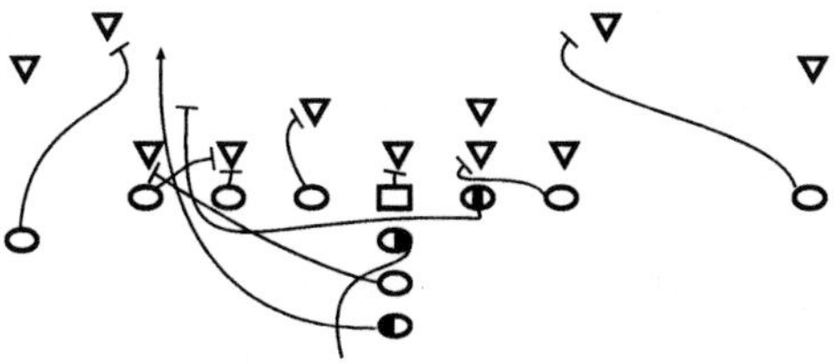

6-6 48 G Power

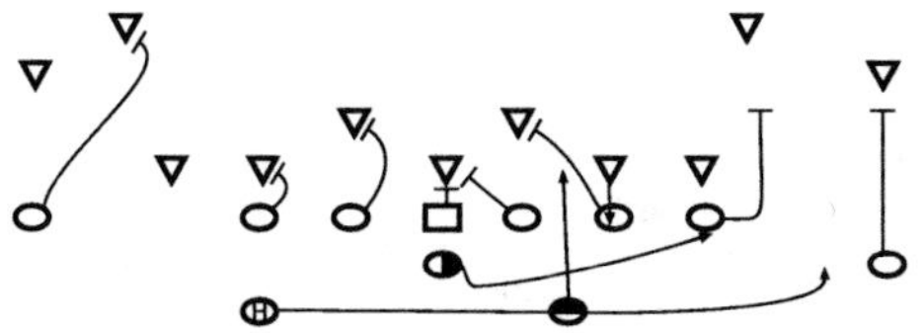

6-7A 41 Dive Option (Triple Option)

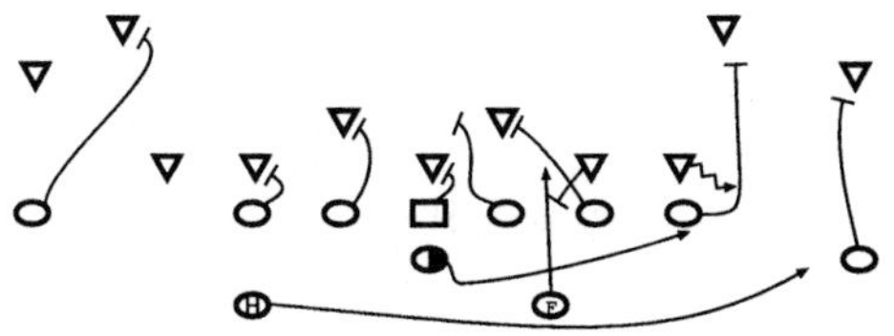

6-7B 41 Dive Option (Triple Option)

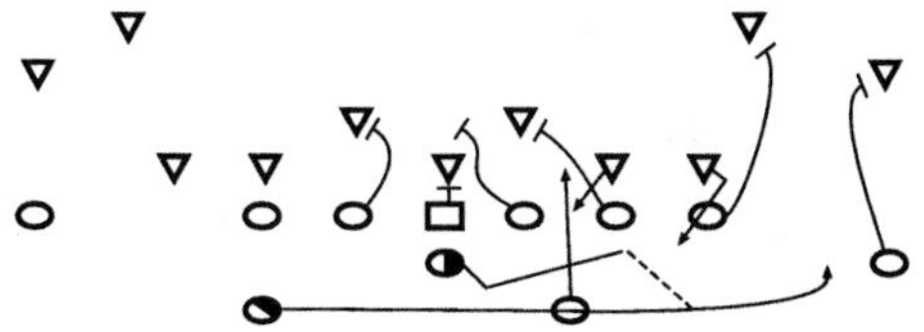

6-7C 41 Dive Option (Triple Option)

The Passing Game

Most football coaches strive to develop balance between running plays and passing plays. In years past, the ratio of running plays to passing plays generally averaged 80 to 20. There has been a trend since the mid-1980s for more teams to approach a 50-50 split. Some throwing teams have been successful despite throwing more passes than attempting runs.

The change in pass protection rules in the mid-1980s enabled offensive linemen liberal use of their hands. This has allowed more time for the quarterback to find an open receiver.

Passing plays are divided into the following categories: drop-back passes; sprint-out and dash passes; play-action passes; and screen passes.

Play-action passes involve the quarterback faking a handoff to the fullback or running back. The back acts as though he has received the ball, buying the quarterback time. If the defenders are fooled, this allows a receiver or back to get open for a pass.

A screen pass involves the quarterback

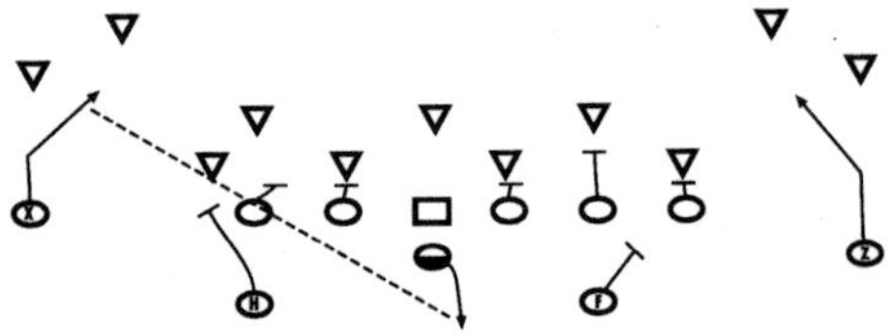

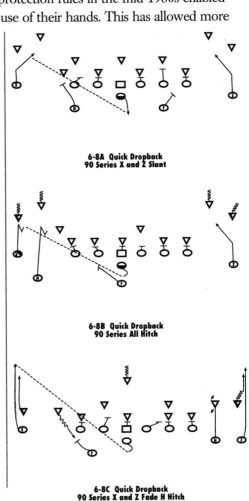

6-8A Quick Dropback
90 Series X and Z Slant

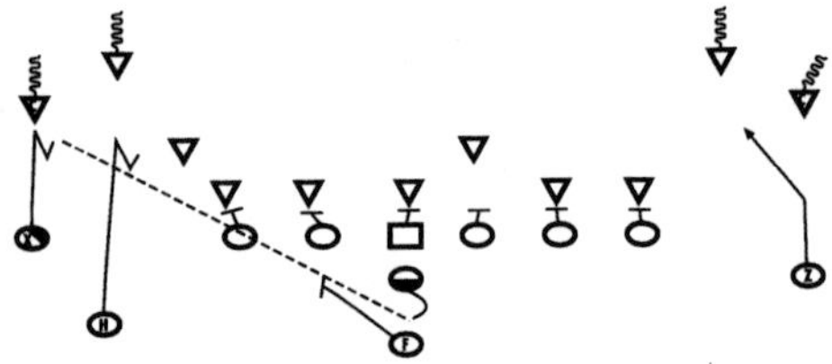

6-8B Quick Dropback
90 Series All Hitch

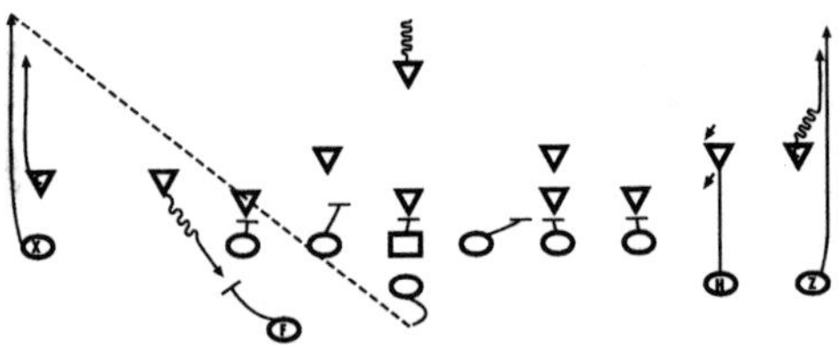

6-8C Quick Dropback
90 Series X and Z Fade H Hitch

dropping back. As he does, a couple of linemen "pull"—or run out to the side—in front of a running back or tight end, who catches the ball at or near the line of scrimmage. The player who catches the ball then follows his blockers up the field. If the defense does not read the screen, big linemen end up blocking fewer, smaller players down field.

Drop-back passes are divided into three categories: quick, intermediate, and deep. Diagrams 6-8A, 6-8B and 6-8C.

Quick drop-back passes involve the quarterback retreating two or three steps. Receivers run short routes and/or fade routes. The offensive linemen and some backs attack defenders aggressively to get their hands down, thus keeping a pass from being knocked down. Most coaches call these types of passes the "90 series."

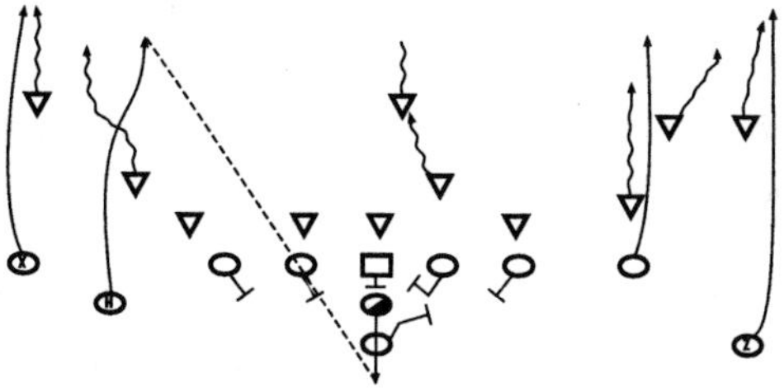

6-9A Intermediate Dropback
OP4 All Take Off

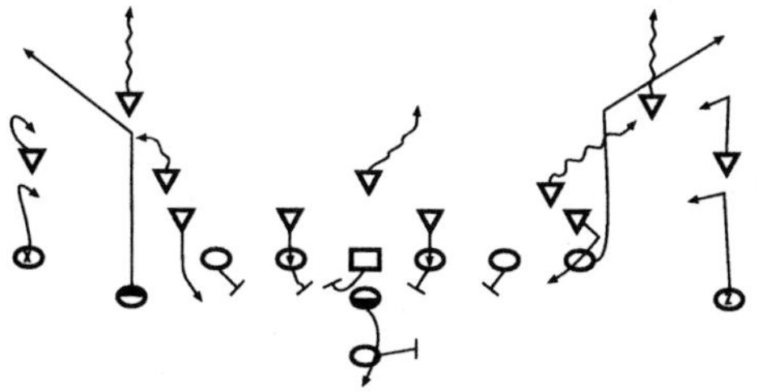

9-6B Intermediate Dropback
OP5 Smash

Diagrams 6-9A and 6-9B. Intermediate drop-back passes involve the quarterback retreating five steps and then throwing the ball. The receivers now can run deeper routes before the ball is thrown. The offensive linemen retreat passively slowing the charge of the defenders with some or all of the backs blocking.

Deep drop-back passes, Diagram 6-11, involve the quarterback retreating seven steps before throwing the ball. The additional depth buys time for the receivers to run deeper, more intricate routes.

Giving the offensive team more time to throw the ball normally results in higher completion percentage, more yardage, more touchdowns and, ultimately, more victories.

Most teams also employ a formation called the shotgun, Diagram 6-12. The quarterback lines up 6 to 8 yards behind the center. Therefore, the quarterback does not have to drop back after taking the ball from the center. However, the ball does have to be centered to the quarterback, and the quarterback must catch the ball before looking downfield. So the center, crouched over the ball, does not simply snap the ball into the quarterback's hands directly. Rather, he snaps it like he would a short version of a punt formation, hiking the ball in the air back to the quarterback. This distance from the defensive linemen allows the quarterback to locate a receiver, as well as providing more space.

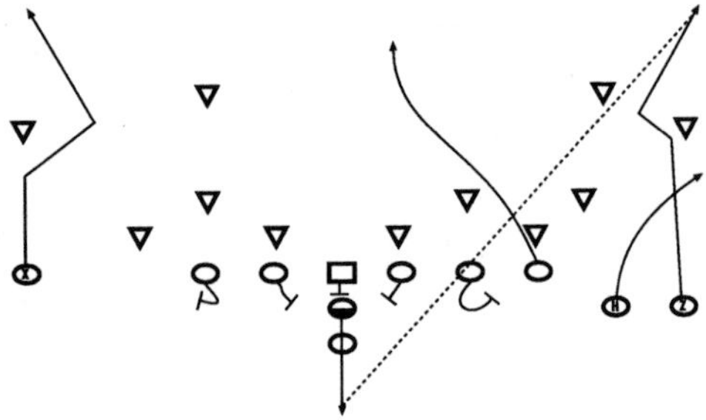

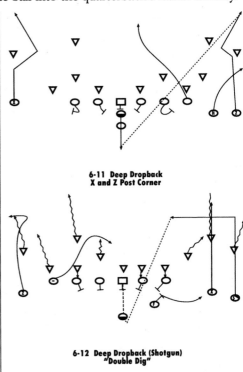

6-11 Deep Dropback
X and Z Post Corner

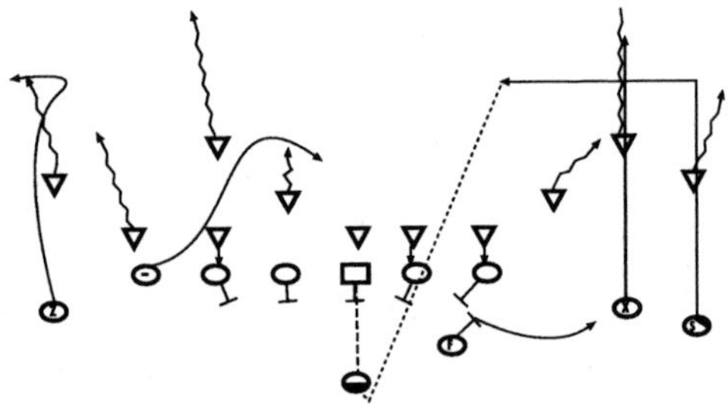

6-12 Deep Dropback (Shotgun)
"Double Dig"

To elude rushing defensive linemen, coaches will employ sprint-out (or roll-out) plays, Diagram 6-13. They are referred to as moving pocket maneuvers (a pocket is a protected area in the offensive backfield where the quarterback sets up to throw a pass) because the quarterback is using the entire pocket to set up a pass, not just the area directly behind the center. The quarterback will run at an angle toward the flank before throwing the ball. The defenders away from the quarterback's maneuver will seldom be able to pressure the passer. Often more time is gained to pass, but the area of the field to which the quarterback can accurately throw is much smaller. Why? Because throwing at an angle is much more difficult.

Another moving pocket maneuver is called a dash pass, Diagram 6-14. The quarterback drops straight back, inviting the rushers to converge on him. Then he runs directly toward the sideline while blockers pin the closest rushers. This maneuver does give the quarterback more time to pass, but as with all these types of plays, the area of the field to which the quarterback can accurately throw is diminished.

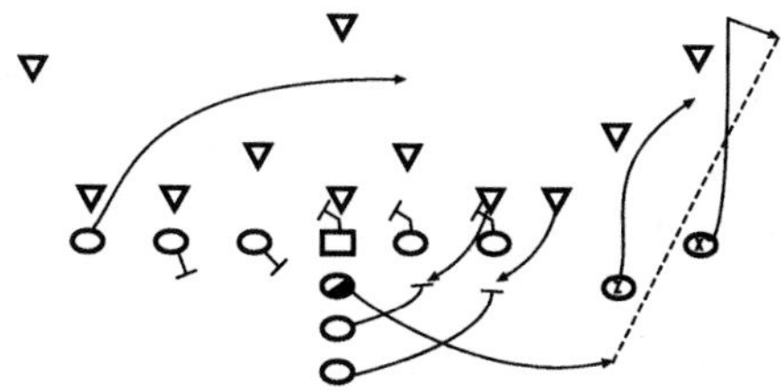

6-13 Sprintout Pass
X and Z Out

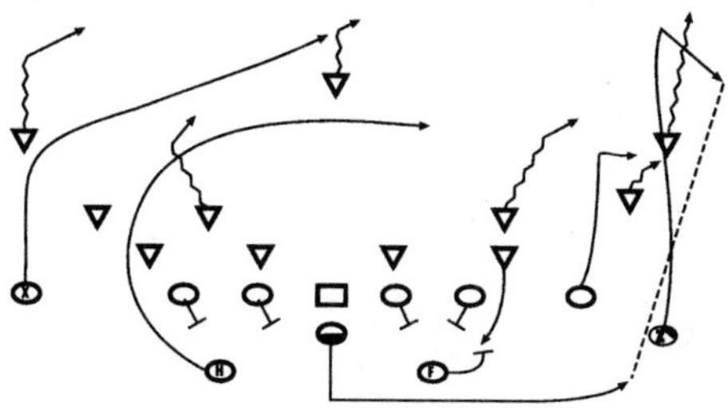

6-14 Dropback Dash Strong

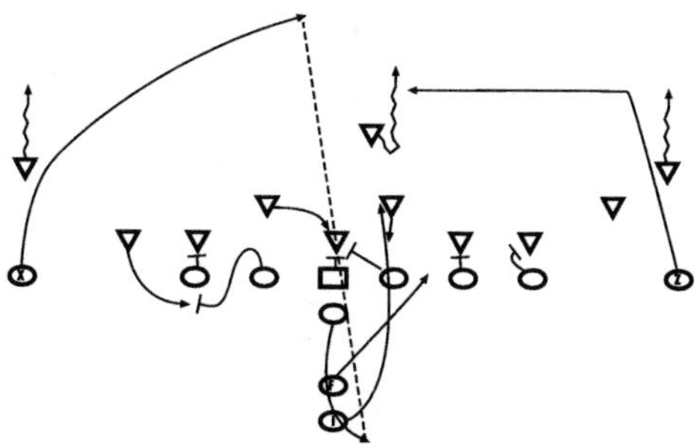

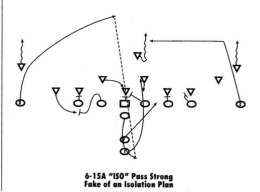

6-15A "ISO" Pass Strong
Fake of an Isolation Plan

Well-conceived play-action passes can be most successful, Diagram 6-15. A running play is faked to freeze some of the defenders. Often more time is gained for the quarterback to throw the ball. If the defenders overreact to a fake to the running back, a receiver can break free for a big gain or even a score.

Generally the University of Nebraska will attempt the fewest passes in the Big 12 Conference yet end the season with the most touchdown passes completed. The more effective a team's run offense, the better their opportunity to successfully throw play-action passes. Great pressure is placed on the defenders to read whether the play is a run or a pass. Often receivers are wide open. A quarterback's accuracy can be off a little, yet the pass can still be completed. However, if the receiver is covered even marginally well, any pass that is significantly off target will likely be either incomplete or intercepted by the opposing team.

The quarterback is not the only player to throw passes. Occasionally a halfback or even a wide receiver will throw the ball. In fact, one of the most difficult play-action passes to stop is a halfback pass thrown back to the quarterback. Defensive teams do not usually account for a quarterback as a receiver.

A wide receiver will throw a pass off a reverse. Defensive backs will often overreact to a reverse, forgetting to cover their assigned receiver. These trick—or "exotic"—plays are seldom used, perhaps once or twice a game at the most. Usually they are used when coaches recognize that the opposing defense has shown a tendency that would allow such a play to succeed. This might involve the defensive players staying too close to the line of scrimmage, or it could mean the defensive team is covering the receivers with only a single defender and no second or third line of defense.

One of the best strategies to offset a tremendous pass rush is to use screen passes. The offensive linemen allow the defensive rushers to beat them on an apparent pass play. Once the defenders get by the offensive linemen, the offensive linemen go to block their assigned men. Thus, the linemen form a screen for the receiver.

A screen pass must be completed behind the line of scrimmage.

Therefore, the linemen are allowed to block downfield attacking the linebackers and defensive backs before the ball is even caught.

A traditional screen pass play involves the quarterback dropping back five steps, pausing, and then dropping back a few steps more, drawing the rushers. The ball is then thrown to the running back who has set up to block and then turned back to receive the ball. The offensive tackle sets up to pass protect, inviting the rusher to drive deep into the backfield. Then the tackle cut blocks the rusher, allowing the halfback to get a running start behind the screen blockers.

In a hide screen, the quarterback fakes a draw play to the running back. After the fake, the running back gets "lost in the crowd." Then he looks back, catches the ball, and runs behind the blockers.

If the screen pass is covered by the defense, the quarterback has the option to throw to the tight end, who is an outlet receiver. The tight end hooks up about eight to 10 yards deep directly over the center.

A most effective screen concept is the double screen. The quarterback has two options. He can throw a quick screen to one side. Or if that is covered, he can throw a middle screen to the opposite side. The double screen concept can be well timed and very difficult to consistently stop. The defenders are split trying to stop both potential receivers.

The middle screen part of the play is called the jail-break screen. It probably is called that because to the few defenders, it looks like a mass of convicts coming at them!

Receivers learn to run various routes to get open to catch passes. The various routes are shown as a tree on the next page.

General Passing Tree

⟵ Sideline - Ball ⟶

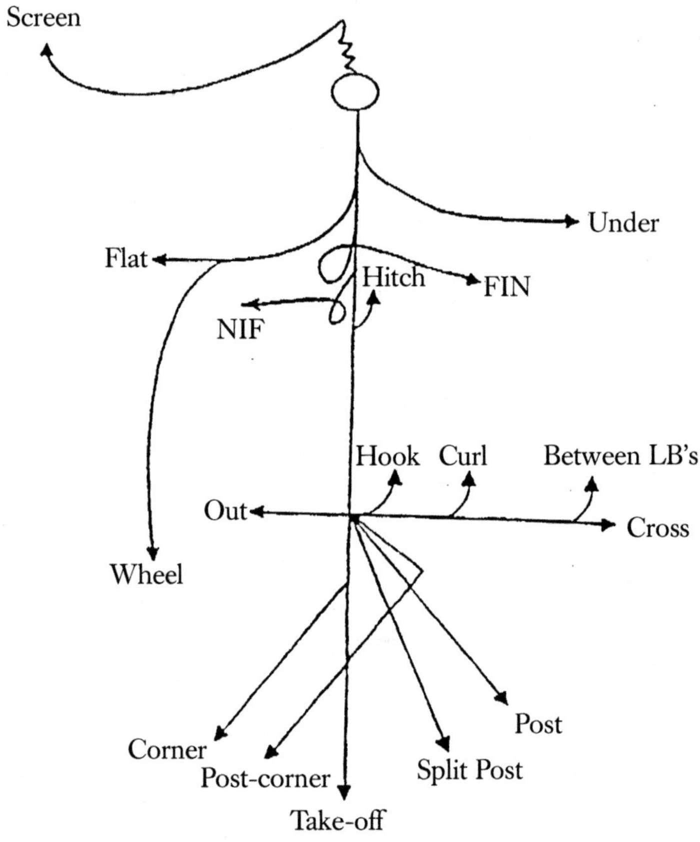

CHAPTER 7

Formations

THE STATE U. SALAMANDERS, PERENNIAL DOORMATS OF THE CONFERENCE, DEVELOP A NATIONAL REPUTATION FOR THEIR WORK IN THE AREA OF INNOVATIVE FORMATIONS...
© PAUL FELL
FORMATION "B-4 CHICKEN CLUSTER"

It may seem amazing that with 11 men, seven of whom must be on the line of scrimmage while on offense, teams can get into literally hundreds of different formations. The prospect of using various alignments to take advantage of personnel strengths, as well as strategy to move the ball in order to defeat an opponent, adds variety to the game.

Normally the offensive team will huddle and receive information vital to the upcoming play. The quarterback will tell his teammates how to line up, what play will be used, and when the ball will be snapped.

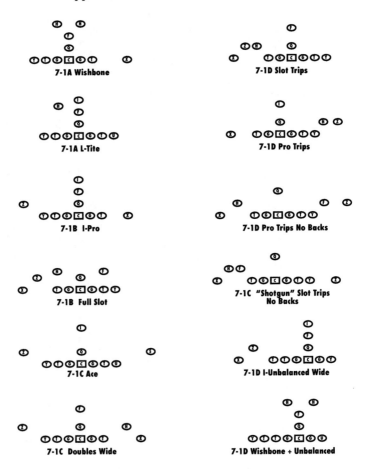

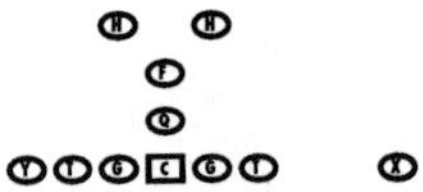
7-1A Wishbone

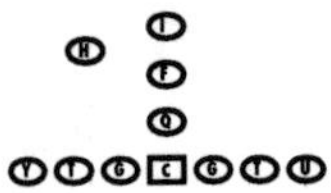
7-1A L-Tite

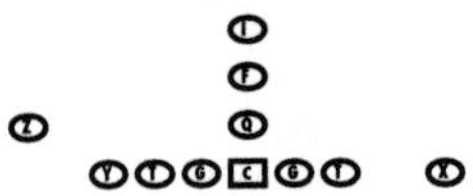
7-1B I-Pro

7-1B Full Slot

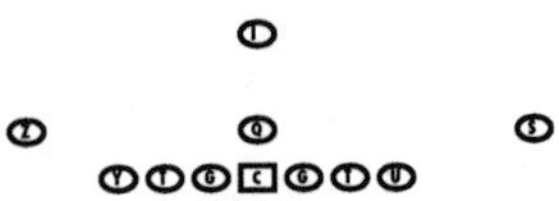
7-1C Ace

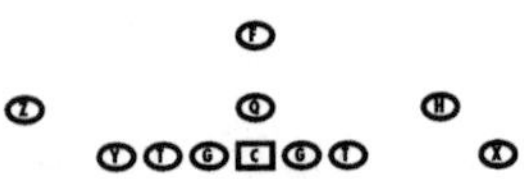
7-1C Doubles Wide

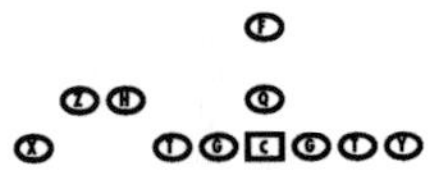
7-1D Slot Trips

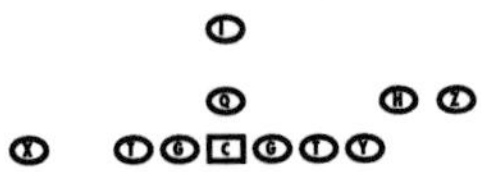
7-1D Pro Trips

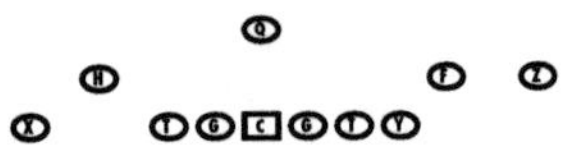
7-1D Pro Trips No Backs

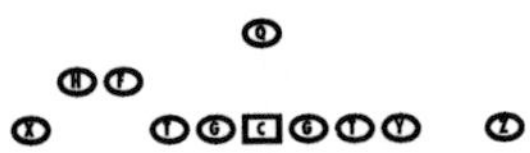
7-1C "Shotgun" Slot Trips No Backs

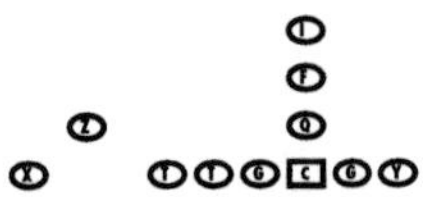
7-1D I-Unbalanced Wide

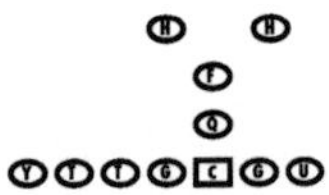
7-1D Wishbone + Unbalanced

Poor adjustments to offensive formations by the defense can allow for some big plays. Offensive coaches attempt to confuse the defense, not only by the use of various formations, but also by shifts and motions.

A way to simplify your understanding of formations is to divide possible sets into six groupings: three-back set, two-back set, one-back, double width, no backs and unbalanced line, Diagram 7-1.

The following pages contain specific formations that fit in these six groupings. Other maneuvers such as "fly" and "motion" are described. Watch the next game to see how many formations the two teams use.

Formation numbering system

Every team has a number system to designate the hole or area to attack—as shown—and the backs. Diagrams 7-2, 7-3.

Some teams number their holes odd numbers on one side, even on the other. The numbers could also be labeled high to low, inside to out, or vice versa.

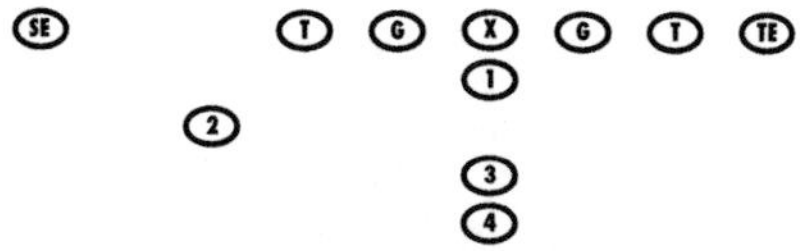

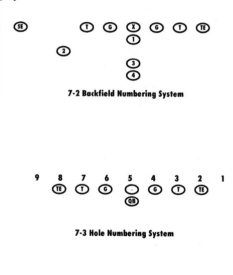

7-2 Backfield Numbering System

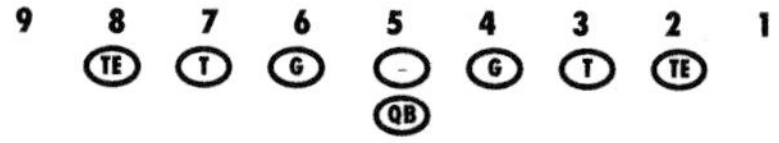

7-3 Hole Numbering System

How a coach designates his holes really doesn't matter. Communication is the key. Using the examples shown in Diagrams 7-2 and 7-3, a play around the right end carried by the I-back would be a 41.

Following the double number would be a descriptive word to explain the blocking scheme. For example, 41 Pitch, Diagram 7-4, would be a play where the quarterback turns and pitches the ball to the I-back who runs the ball to his right with specific blocking assignments for the other players.

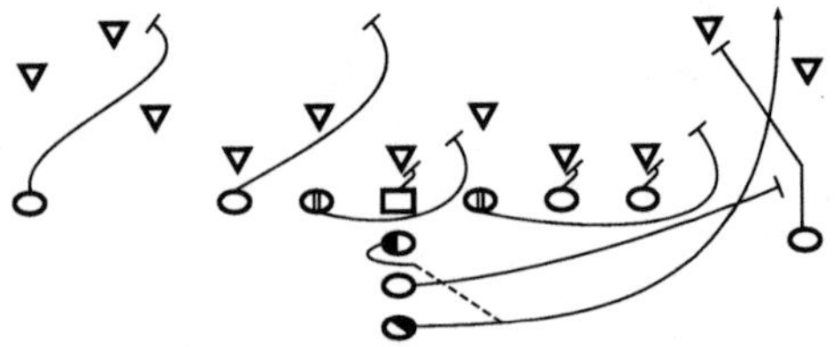

7-4 41 Pitch

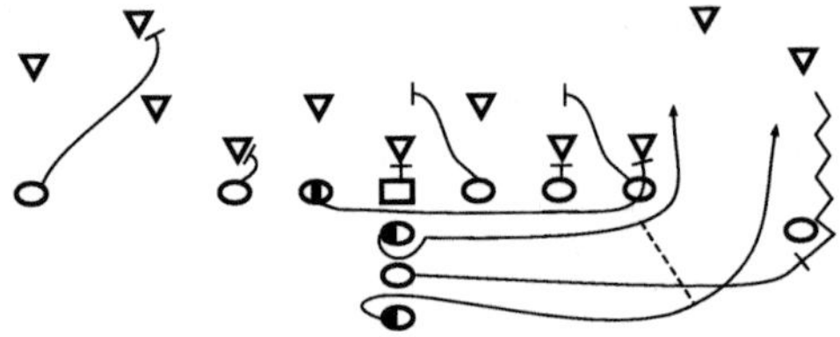

7-5 41 Sprint

A 41 Sprint, Diagram 7-5, would be an option play where the quarterback would run laterally to his right, hoping to draw the defense to him. He would then pitch the ball to the I-back, or keep it himself if they failed to honor him.

A 37 Dive, Diagram 7-6, would be a handoff to the fullback toward the seven hole. The quarterback would pivot and hand the ball to the fullback. The linemen would apply their blocking rules against the

defensive alignment. The quarterback and I-back would continue around to the left, hoping to draw some of the defense with them.

Many plays can be run out of numerous formations. The offensive team at the point of attack can execute their blocking patterns regardless of where the rest of the team aligns.

Some coaches package their running plays into series. The backfield action will be exactly the same. However, the ball will be handed off to a back as designated by the middle number. The last number will signify the hole to be attacked with a descriptive word or words to instruct the linemen and ends as to their blocking assignments.

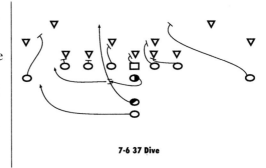

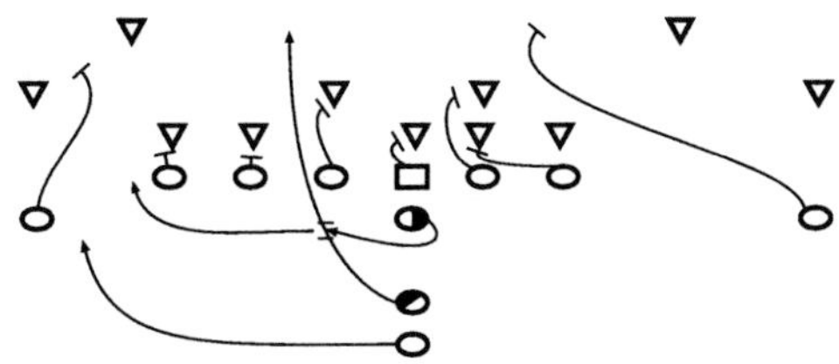

7-6 37 Dive

In this system, play-action passes can be run as the players fake into designated holes.

I WAS WONDERING IF MY FAMILIARITY WITH OFFENSIVE AND DEFENSIVE TERMINOLOGY MIGHT BE USED AS CREDIT TOWARD THE FOREIGN LANGUAGE REQUIREMENT..?
ACADEMIC ADVISING

CHAPTER 8

Defense

A strong defensive team is a vital part of a solid football team. By minimizing the points allowed, as well as by minimizing the first downs gained, the offensive team will have more chances to score, since they will have the ball more often (time of possession).

A good defensive performance often includes gaining turnovers (interceptions and fumble recoveries), scoring points, and gaining great field position for the offense.

I believe the statement "Offense sells tickets, but defense wins championships" points to the value and necessity of a solid defensive team.

Actually all phases of the game are important—kicking, defense and offense. However, a great number of games are won with an excellent defense, excellent kicking and an average offense. A great offense with an average defense and an adequate kicking game has not proven to be as successful.

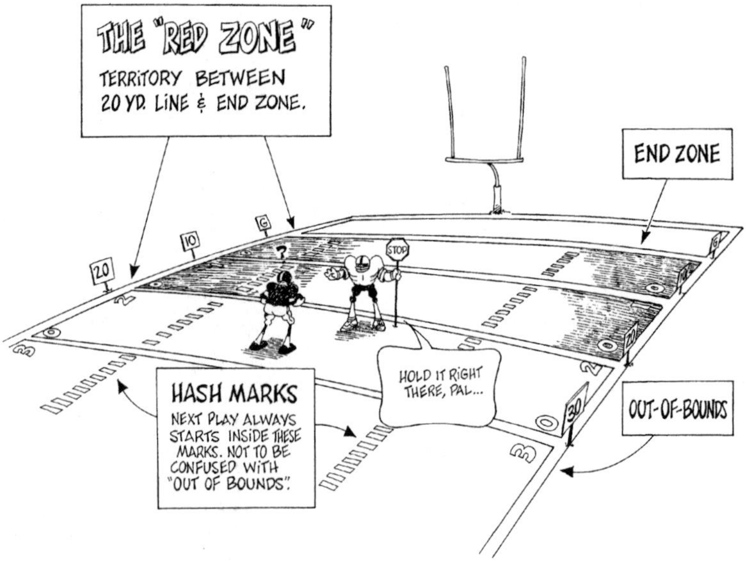

Some priorities that defensive teams strive to achieve might include the following:

1. Holding the opponent to less than 3.0 yards average per rush.
2. Intercepting at least one out of every 17 passes.
3. Holding the opponent to 285 total yards (running and passing) or less during a game.
4. Holding the opponent to 13 points or less.
5. Gaining three or more turnovers (interceptions, fumble recoveries) per game.
6. Stopping 70 percent of third-down plays from achieving a first down, thus forcing fourth downs (situations when the team must usually punt the ball).
7. Holding the opponent to less than two yards per attempt 60 percent of the time.
8. Preventing the opponent from scoring a touchdown 70 percent of the time inside the "Red Zone" (from your 20-yard line to the goal line).

Other goals also might be set by individual schools.

Most college defensive teams will base out of a 5-2 front or a 4-3 alignment. A coach will make this decision considering the abilities of the players available and/or his coaching philosophy. Also, defensive alignments used by successful teams are copied.

A wise coach will play defenses that utilize the skills of the players available rather than get caught up in trends. These choices are vital to get the greatest production out of the team.

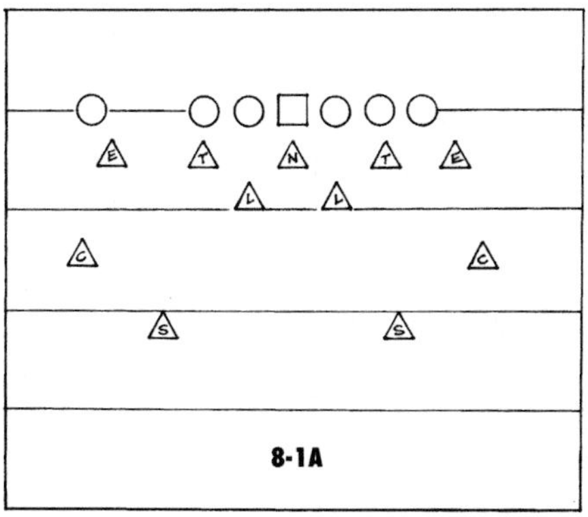

A 5-2 defensive alignment simply involves the use of five defensive linemen, two linebackers, and four defensive backs. Diagram 8-1A.

A 3-4 alignment involves three defensive linemen, four linebackers and four defensive backs, Diagram 8-1B.

A 5-3 defense uses five defensive linemen, three linebackers and three defensive backs, Diagram 8-1C.

A 4-3 defense uses four defensive linemen, three linebackers and four defensive backs, Diagram 8-1D.

The first order of business is for the defensive players to perform techniques to defeat the offensive blocking scheme, tackle the ball carrier, and/or cover the receivers. Regardless of how a defensive team aligns, the players have responsibilities that cover running plays as well as passing plays.

The area between two offensive linemen or outside the ends is known commonly as a "gap." The defensive team strives to be able to stop a running play through any gap.

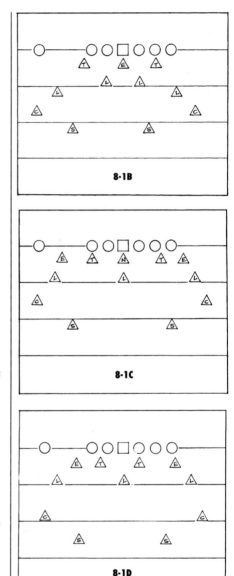

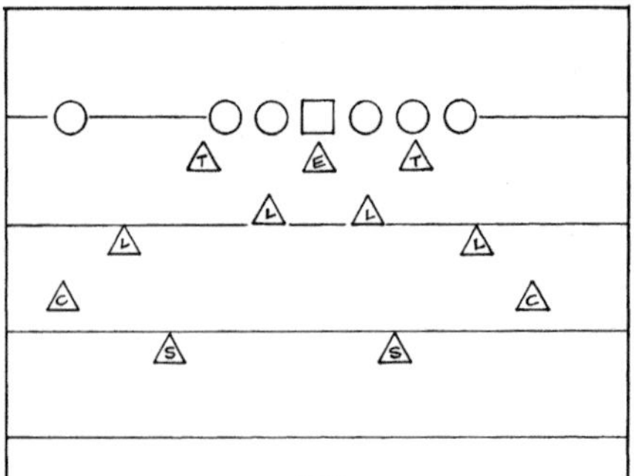

8-1B

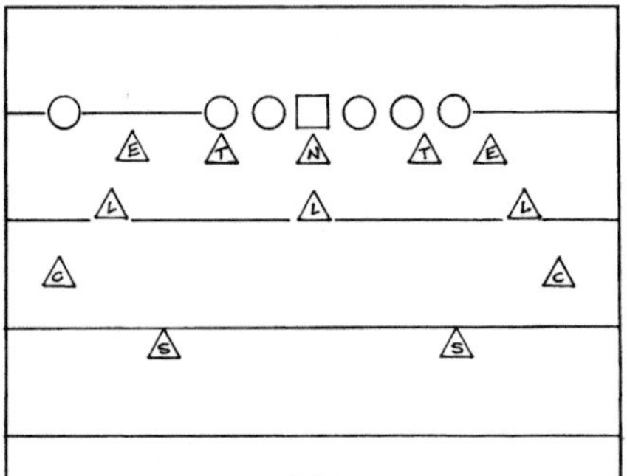

8-1C

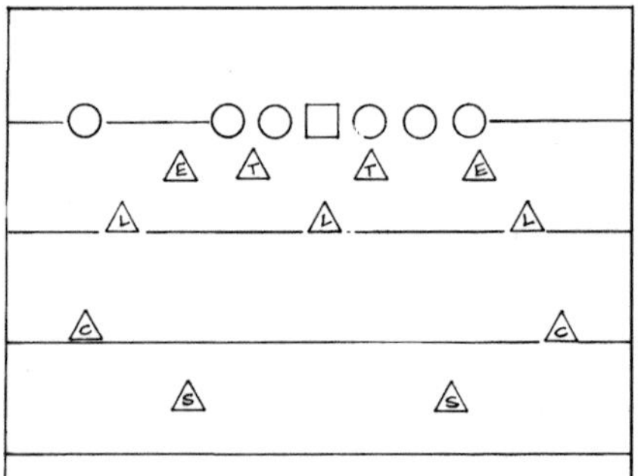

8-1D

Therefore, gap integrity is of vital importance. Most players will be assigned a gap for which they are responsible. If the defense can control the gap, then the running back must attempt to go elsewhere or be tackled, Diagram 8-2.

Some players on the defensive team are given the responsibility of covering two gaps. A middle guard ("nose tackle" in NFL jargon) aligned head on the center may have to tackle the ball carrier in either One Gap or A Gap (right or left), depending on whether numbers or letters identify gaps, Diagram 8-3.

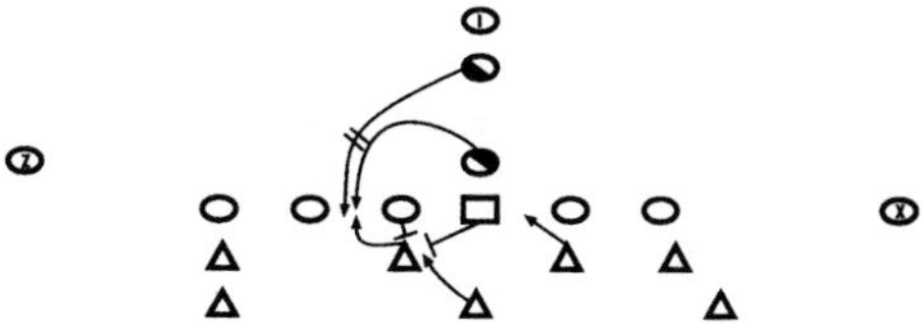

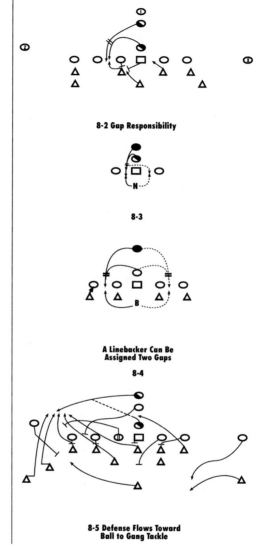

8-2 Gap Responsibility

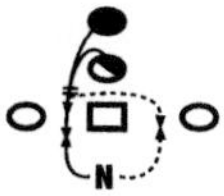

8-3

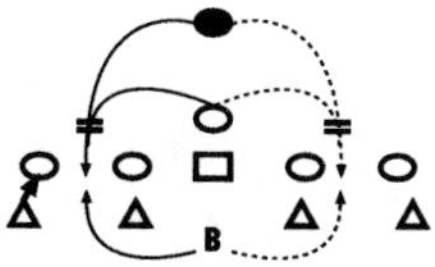

A Linebacker Can Be Assigned Two Gaps

8-4

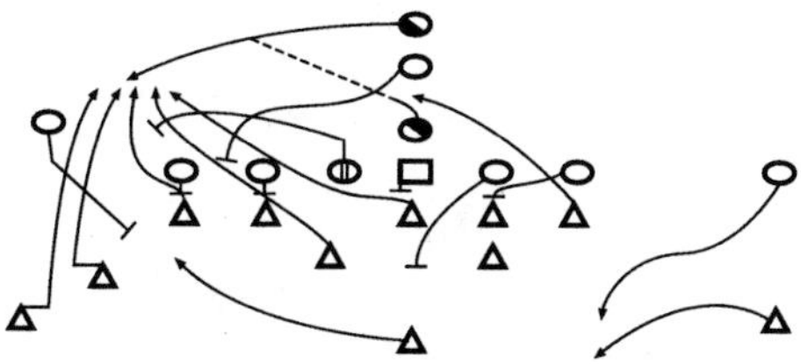

8-5 Defense Flows Toward Ball to Gang Tackle

In the event that a linebacker is assigned two gaps and play starts to one side, he is responsible for covering the gap closer to the ball, Diagram 8-4.

Once each player handles his initial responsibility, all players on a good defensive team will pursue toward the ball. The better defensive football teams seldom have only one player making a tackle. "Gang tackling" is the ideal. It is very discouraging for a running back or receiver to be hit by numerous opponents. It takes a toll and often can be the key factor in which team performs better in the fourth quarter. In a close ball game this also may be the key to winning or losing, Diagram 8-5.

All 11 defensive players are ultimately responsible for stopping a running play; however, some defensive backs are the last line of defense and should seldom make tackles on a running play.

Also, all defensive team members are responsible for defeating the opponent's pass offense.

Some of the players (generally the defensive tackles, ends and nose guard) are responsible for rushing the quarterback on passing plays.

Ideally, they hope to tackle him before he can pass, which is known as a "sack," or at least cause him to rush his throw and/or tip the pass. Relentless pursuit of the quarterback is the starting point in controlling and defeating the opponent's pass offense.

The rest of the defenders (usually linebackers and defensive backs) will employ one of three possible types of coverage to defeat the quarterback's ability to find an open receiver. The first option is for the defensive team to "blitz" six men and cover the five receivers "man-to-man" with the other five defenders. By rushing more men, it is possible to "sack" the quarterback or at least give him little time to throw the football. The man-to-man defenders receive no help past the line of scrimmage; they must cover an assigned individual receiver. They count on the strong rush to force quick, errant throws or sacks.

The goal is to have the play last less than three seconds from the time the ball is snapped. If the rushing defenders allow over three seconds for the pass to find an open receiver, the likelihood of a complete pass and substantial yardage gained is greatly increased. Man-to-man is the most difficult coverage for a defender because he is trying to cover a speedy receiver who knows where he is going. The receiver tries to defeat the defense by faking or masking his intended route.

The second way to defend against the pass is to rush three or four men and have all the other players drop into a "zone." Regardless of where the receivers go, the defenders protect their turf. Whereas man-to-man defense requires the defender to focus strictly on the assigned receiver, zone coverage requires the defender to focus on his assigned area of the field and the "eyes" of the quarterback (actually his head and shoulders).

When the quarterback takes his front hand off the ball every pass defender should "break" or sprint in the direction he is throwing. By reading the quarterback's intention, a defender can cover a large area even if more than one receiver is in it. When all defenders break to the ball, they shrink the seams between zones, making it difficult for a pass to be completed.

It is generally perceived more interceptions occur when playing a zone coverage. The focus on the quarterback allows a better "jump" on the ball. It can also be seen from the time it leaves the passer's hand.

Fewer interceptions happen in man-to-man coverage, but the opponent's pass-completion percentage should be less. This is because defenders are very close to the man they are covering.

Diagrams 8-6A and 8-6B show "two deep" and "three deep" zone coverages:

In the "two deep" zone coverage, the safeties must literally be able to handle any deep throw in their half of the field over 15 yards to the goal line.

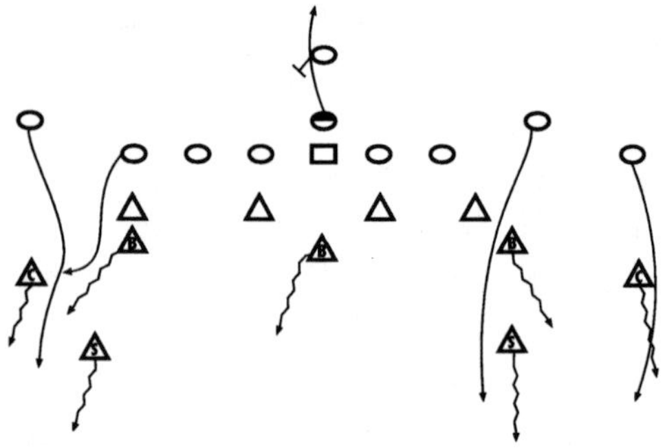

8-6A Two Deep Zone

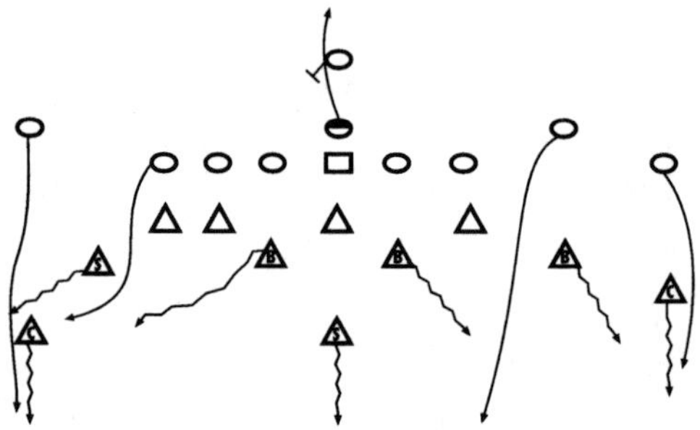

8-6B Three Deep Zone

The other five defenders divide the field into fifths. Each defender covering his zone makes it more difficult for short passes to be completed. (Note: Good zone teams will also have defenders cheat out of their zone if there is no threat, thus helping the deep defender.) An example is as follows:

In the "three deep" zone coverage, three defensive backs divide the field into thirds. They are responsible for handling all throws over 15 yards to the goal line in their third. Normally, four other defenders (a defensive back and three linebackers) divide the area 15 yards past the line of scrimmage into fourths.

Occasionally, a team will rush only three men, put three men in the deep zone and divide the short area between the remaining five defenders. Although it is easier to defend deep passes out of a three deep zone coverage, there are more seams between short and deep areas.

The third means of defending against a pass offensive is to design "combination" coverages that include elements of man-to-man techniques and zone techniques. Generally five defenders will cover the five eligible receivers man-to-man, while two other defenders will cover two zones. A variety of these coverages can be designed. One popular hybrid is two zone players in deep zone with five others playing man-to-man. Diagram 8-7.

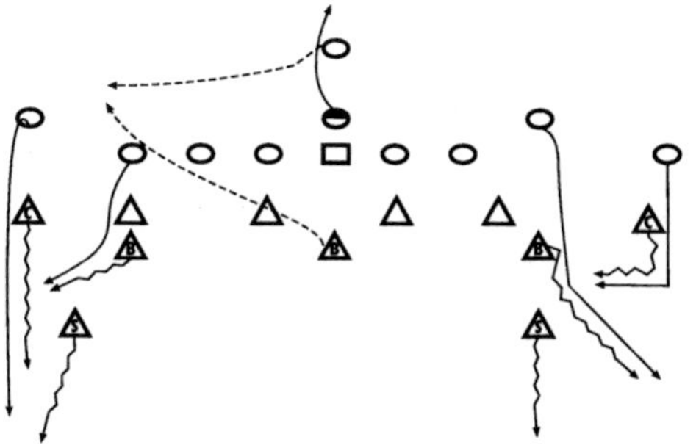

8-7 D8

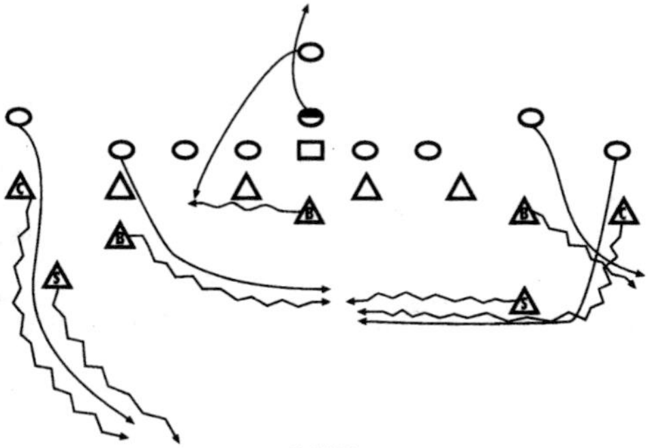

8-8 D9

A second popular combination is for two zone defenders to cover the middle of the field and five others to cover man-to-man, Diagram 8-8.

Combination coverages are popular because they incorporate tight man-to-man coverage with the safety of two zone players protecting them. Thus, there is some security in not giving up the "big play."

Each pass coverage and each defense employed has strengths and weaknesses. It is the job of the defensive coaches to have a variety of defensive maneuvers to handle the most complex offenses. Coaches are constantly striving to be creative and come up with "new wrinkles" to confound and stymie offensive attacks and vice versa.

One of the most creative developments in defensive football has been the advent of "zone blitzes." These maneuvers have come out of the NFL and have been most utilized by the Pittsburgh Steelers and Carolina Panthers. Whereas traditional blitzes have included strict man-to-man coverage, zone blitzes allow for good pressure, but safer coverage—it creates a sort of "have your cake and eat it, too" scenario, Diagram 8-9.

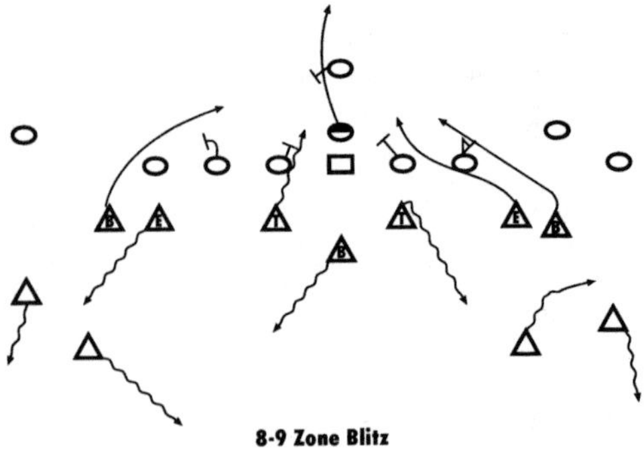

8-9 Zone Blitz

Once an opponent gets inside the defensive team's 20-yard line (red zone), the defensive team must keep the opponent out of the end zone to be successful. If the defensive team chooses to play zone defenses against the pass, the area to cover is much smaller. Some teams facing a passing play will only rush three men while dropping eight men into zones.

Other teams will choose a variety of blitzes in hopes of causing negative yards. Again, the defenders do not have to cover the receivers for great distances due to the field position.

Once the opponent gets inside the five- or six-yard line, many teams substitute big linemen for defensive backs in hopes of stopping the offense's goal-line attack. Offensive plays to stop (in order of importance) in this area of the field are: quarterback sneak; fullback dive; I-back isolation; pitch sweep; and play-action pass. They are defined in Diagrams 8-10A, 8-10B, 8-10C, 8-10D and 8-10E.

Quarterback sneak: The quarterback, lined up directly under the center, takes the ball and bulls his way forward.

Fullback dive: The quarterback takes the snap and hands it to the fullback, who charges straight ahead or dives through the line of scrimmage.

I-back isolation: The purpose is to block at the line of scrimmage and force a linebacker to make a solo stop on the I-back.

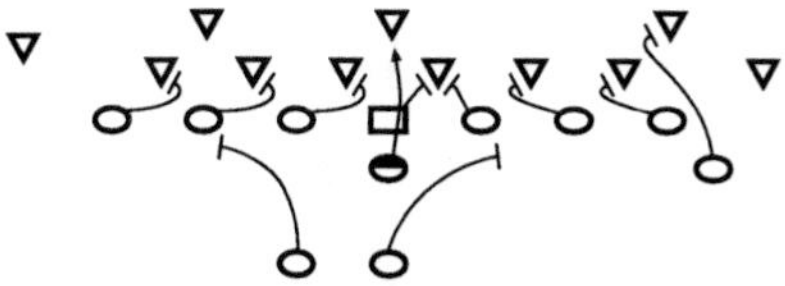

8-10A 15 Smash

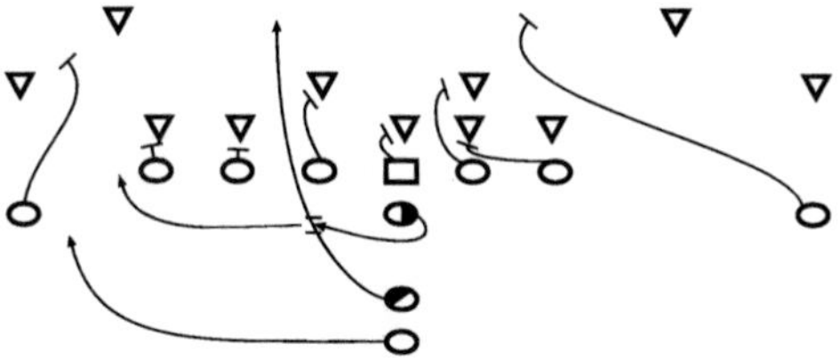

8-10B 37 Dive

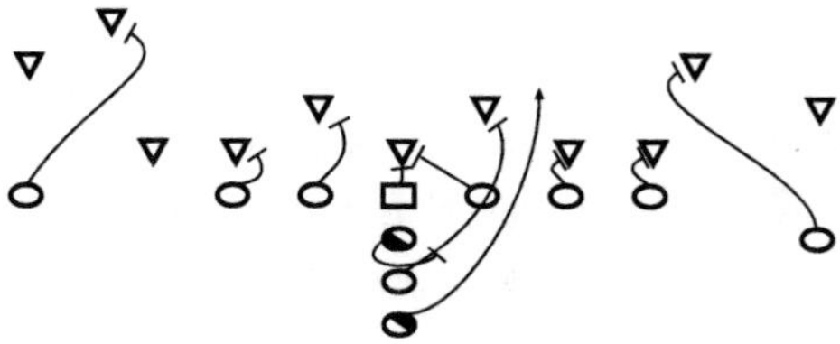

8-10C 44 Isolation

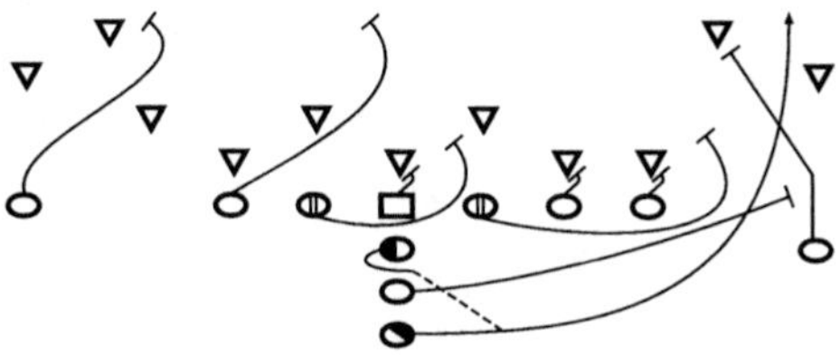

8-10D 41 Pitch

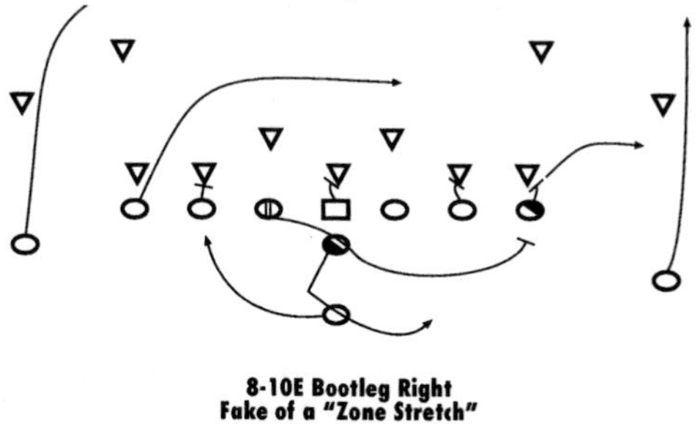

8-10E Bootleg Right
Fake of a "Zone Stretch"

Thus if the I-back can beat this one man—and everyone else takes care of their responsibilities there is potential for a significant gain.

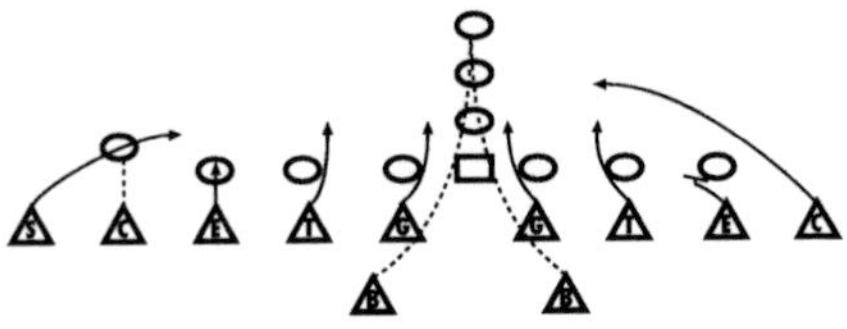

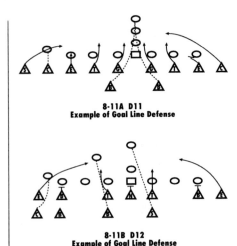

8-11A D11
Example of Goal Line Defense

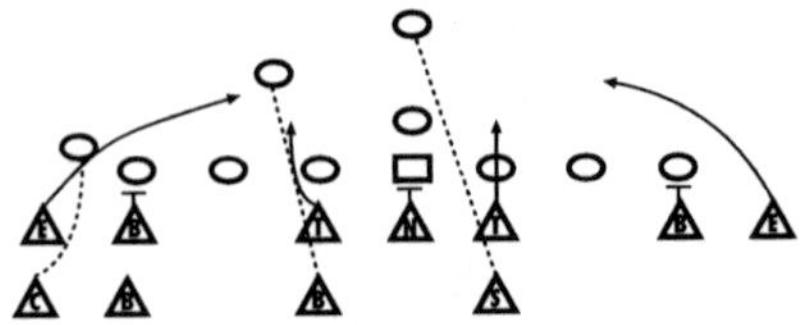

8-11B D12
Example of Goal Line Defense

Pitch sweep: The quarterback takes the snap and the linemen, fullback and receivers block to a designated side. The running back takes a pitch from the quarterback and follows his blockers, who are pushing the defenders either backward, out of the way, or both.

Play-action pass: The quarterback fakes a handoff to the fullback or running back, who act as though they have the ball and crash into the line of scrimmage. This is to fool the defense. The quarterback then tries to throw a quick pass to a receiver, end or back. If the defensive backs and linebackers are also fooled, they might leave a receiver, tight end or back uncovered.

The defensive team must penetrate to stop the offense for losses. Ideally the defense can force a "turnover," or at least force the opponent to attempt a field goal. Examples of goal line defenses are shown in Diagrams 8-11A and 8-11B.

At one time in the college game, one platoon football was played. Athletes played both an offensive position and a defensive position. For example, the quarterback would also play safety, the running back became a defensive back, and the center covered a linebacker position.

In the 1950s the rules were modified for limited substitution. Players could be in and out of the game a limited number of times per half. Therefore practices were divided in some manner so that a player worked on his offensive skills and his defensive skills. There were fewer offensive formations and plays and fewer defenses. On game day, the fans would see little variety and players with specific talents seldom got to play when the outcome of the game was in doubt.

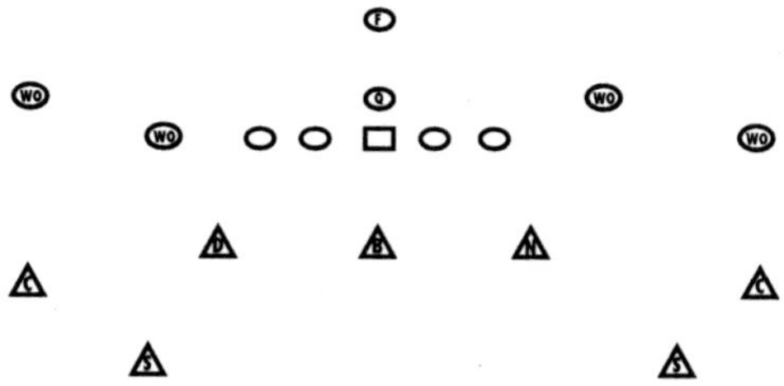

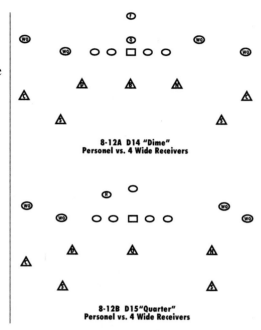

8-12A D14 "Dime" Personel vs. 4 Wide Receivers

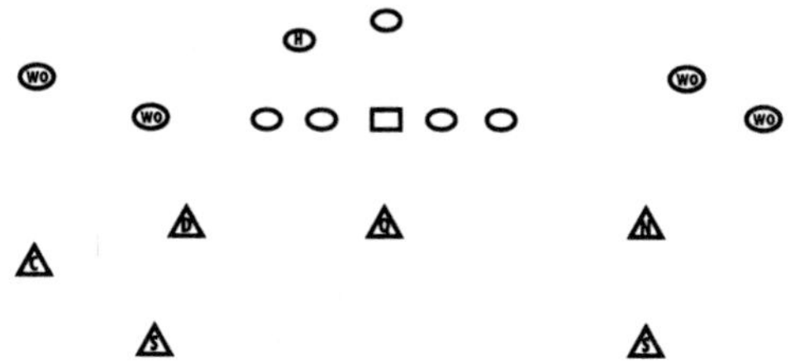

8-12B D15"Quarter" Personel vs. 4 Wide Receivers

In today's era of specialization, the player who has specific talents, but possibly limited overall talent, can be an integral part of the team. For example, a player might be slight of build, but possess great ability to return kicks. Desmond Howard, a reserve receiver for the Green Bay Packers, was selected as the Most Valuable Player in the 1997 Super Bowl win over New England. His tremendous kick returns were deemed to be the key plays in the win.

Today the college level is packed with a tremendous variety of offenses and defenses. Hundreds of formations and plays executed by talented athletes increase the excitement of the game. The NFL defensive coaches lead the way in matching up defensive personnel to their offensive counterparts, as well as changing players due to down and distance of the next play.

There were always changes in goal-line personnel, but now we have "nickel, dime, and quarter" personnel. In a "nickel" defense, a defensive back substitutes for a linebacker to provide better pass coverage. On "dime" and "quarter" defenses, two and three defensive backs, respectively, replace linebackers, Diagrams 8-12A and 8-12B.

CHAPTER 9

The Kicking Game *(includes all special teams)*

The least appreciated and least understood phase of football is the kicking game—which really does not make sense when you consider that the sport is called "foot" ball!

Every close game is won or lost in the kicking game whether it be by an extra point (also known as a PAT) or field goals, by the yardage gained on punts, kickoffs and returns, or the field position (and points) gained by blocked kicks. Formations for kickoffs, punts, field goals and point-after attempts, which begin at the three-yard line, are shown in Diagrams 9-1, 9-2, 9-3 and 9-4.

Many coaches feel that great defense and kicking games translate into championships. In the 1995 Orange Bowl versus the favored Miami Hurricanes, the Cornhuskers dominated the kicking game and won their third national championship. Miami fumbled a punt-return attempt and snapped the ball over the punter's head, losing tremendous field position. Meanwhile, Husker kicker Darin Erstad constantly kept Miami deep in its own territory with phenomenal punts and kickoffs. While Husker quarterback Tommie Frazier won the Most Valuable Player award for the game with a gutsy and inspired performance, it could be argued that Erstad's performance was the key to victory. A crucial win over No. 3 Colorado earlier that year also was sealed by Erstad's punting and kicking.

Florida State University has won many games in the last few years by blocking opponent's punt attempts. Not only have they scored on many of the blocked kicks, but at the very least they have gained great field position for FSU's offense.

Another great aspect of the kicking game is that younger or less skilled players cut their teeth on kicking teams. They can get valuable playing time while helping their team achieve success.

The beginning of every half of the game begins with a kickoff. Usually, but not always, one team will kick off to start the game, and the other team will kick off to start the second half.

A team could win the toss prior to the game and choose to defer until the second half. The loser of the toss could elect to receive.

Prior to the second half, the winner of the toss could choose to kick off again. This seldom happens. However, weather, especially wind conditions and the strength of one's defensive team, could dictate this strategy. In addition, there is a kickoff after every score. Barring a penalty or a kickoff following a "safety," (a safety occurs when the offense is tackled in the opponent's endzone), the ball will be kicked off from the 40-yard line (high school), the 35-yard line (college), or the 30-yard line (NFL).

The kicker can place the ball or a tee anywhere from one hash mark to the other. Normally, the ball will be kicked from the middle of the field or near one hash or the other. The receiving

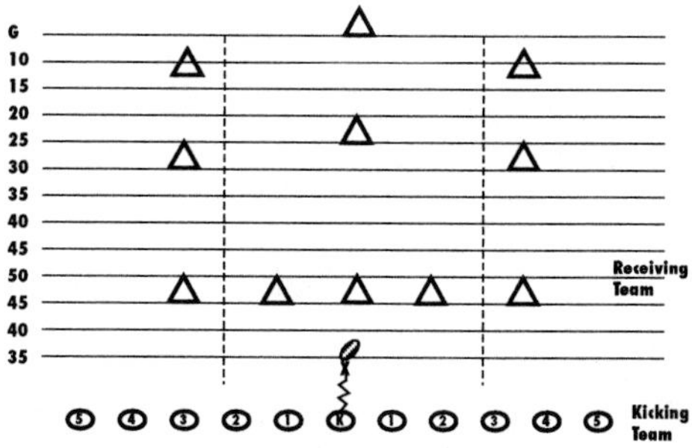

9-1 Formation for Both Kicking and Receiving on Kickoffs

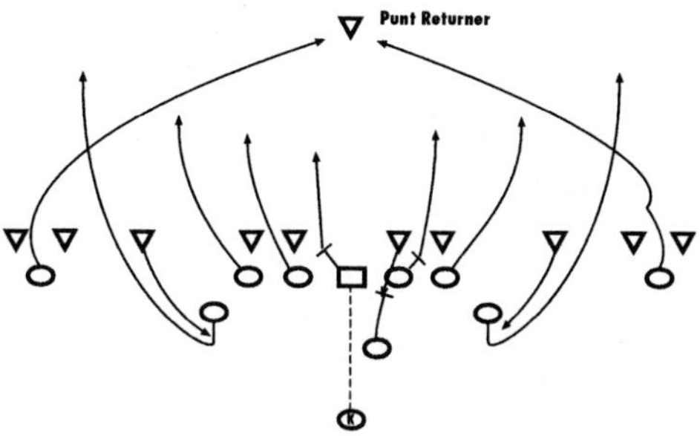

9-2 Punt Formation and Coverage

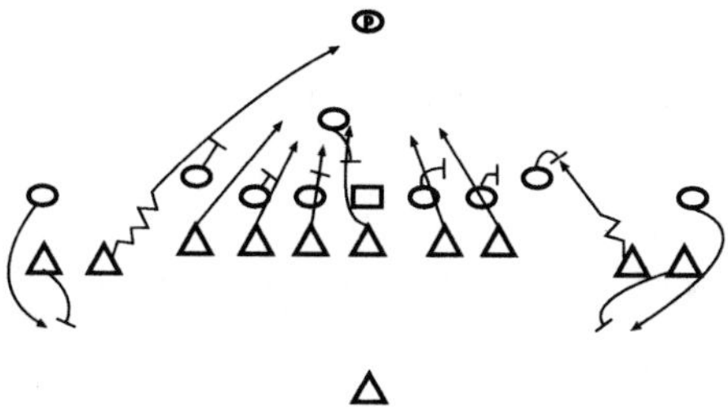

9-3 Punt Block

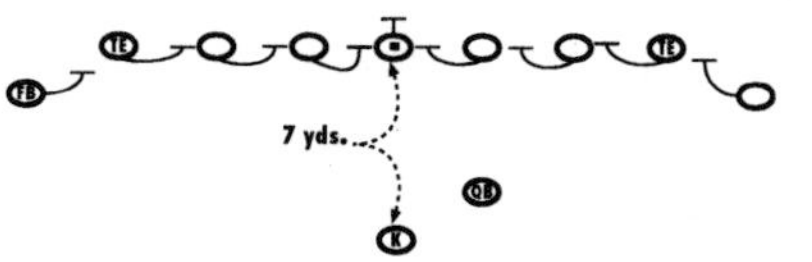

9-3 Extra Points & Field Goals

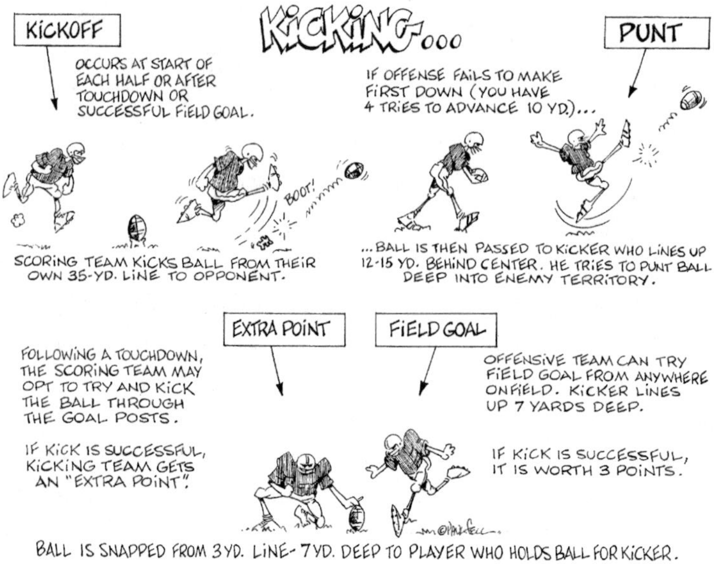

KICKING...
KICKOFF
OCCURS AT START OF EACH HALF OR AFTER TOUCHDOWN OR SUCCESSFUL FIELD GOAL.
BOOT!
SCORING TEAM KICKS BALL FROM THEIR OWN 35-YD. LINE TO OPPONENT.
PUNT
IF OFFENSE FAILS TO MAKE FIRST DOWN (YOU HAVE 4 TRIES TO ADVANCE 10 YD.)...
...BALL IS THEN PASSED TO KICKER WHO LINES UP 12-15 YD. BEHIND CENTER. HE TRIES TO PUNT BALL DEEP INTO ENEMY TERRITORY.
EXTRA POINT
FIELD GOAL
FOLLOWING A TOUCHDOWN, THE SCORING TEAM MAY OPT TO TRY AND KICK THE BALL THROUGH THE GOAL POSTS.
IF KICK IS SUCCESSFUL, KICKING TEAM GETS AN "EXTRA POINT".
OFFENSIVE TEAM CAN TRY FIELD GOAL FROM ANYWHERE ON FIELD. KICKER LINES UP 7 YARDS DEEP.
IF KICK IS SUCCESSFUL, IT IS WORTH 3 POINTS.
BALL IS SNAPPED FROM 3 YD. LINE- 7 YD. DEEP TO PLAYER WHO HOLDS BALL FOR KICKER.

team can line up no closer than 10 yards from the kicking team.

Following a safety, the "guilty" team must kick off from the 20-yard line. The ball can be kicked off a tee on the ground or punted. A reason for punting the ball is to get more hang time to allow the cover team to close with the return man more quickly.

If the kicking team has a strong-legged kicker, they normally will try to kick the ball deep in the end zone forcing the receiving team to down the ball. The ball will then be placed on the 20-yard line following the touchback.

However, some coaches instruct their kicker to kick the ball very high coming down around the goal line. They desire to cover the kick quickly and to tackle the kick-off return man inside the 20-yard line. Obviously, you need a very talented and consistent kicker and aggressive cover men to use this strategy successfully.

A third strategy used to neutralize a great kick-off return man is to "pooch" kick the ball high and somewhat short, forcing a fair catch. The offensive player is unable to advance a fair catch. Ideally, the ball will be caught on or inside the 30-yard line, thus not losing too much field position.

Kicking teams often will set a goal to keep the return team's average starting position inside a certain point, i.e. 23-yard line. The receiving team will use an organized return in an attempt to gain as much yardage as possible. Goals will be set to reach a certain average each game, i.e. 28-yard line.

One standard return is known as a wedge return. Players retreat following the kick, get shoulder to shoulder at a set point and then attack forward blocking the covering team. They hope to open a seam for the kickoff return man.

The second standard return is to attack one side or the other (side return). Various blocking schemes are used. If the covering team converges too quickly, a side return can be most effective.

When a team finds itself behind late in the game following a score, they normally will attempt an onside kick in the hopes of gaining the ball. If they fail, the receiving team gains very good field position. However, the chance must be taken in order to have any opportunity to win.

The onside attempt is normally kicked from one hash or the other. The kicker will "top" the ball with his cleats to make the ball take a big bounce into the air, giving his teammates a chance to recover the ball. The ball must travel at least 10 yards before the recovering team can gain possession. Usually most of the kickoff team shifts outside the hash mark to get into position to gain the ball. The receiving team counters with the "hands" team (generally all receivers and backs, who are used to handling the ball). They can catch the ball either before or after it goes 10 yards. Usually there is a mad scramble attempting to recover the onside kick.

Following a touchdown, the scoring team can attempt to kick for one additional point, a point-after touchdown (PAT) or attempt a run or pass to gain two points. If they attempt a PAT, the ball will be snapped from the three-yard line, placed on the ground at a prescribed distance by the holder (usually 6 to 7 yards deep) and then kicked. A competent kicker will seldom miss a PAT. Therefore, even though a two-point play will reap more points, the consistent PAT is attempted most of the time. The odds are in the favor of kicking unless it is late in the game, and a two-point play is needed to tie or to win.

Starting in 1997, after the second overtime period in a tie game, a scoring team must attempt a two-point play. The aim is to shorten the duration of an overtime game.

The offensive linemen and wingback seal off their inside seam to stop penetration by the defense. Sometimes a wingback will be forced to "double bump." He must hit the inside rusher and then bump to an outside rusher.

A field-goal attempt, worth three points, is possible anytime the defense has stopped a third-down play or time is running out at the end of the half or game. The procedure is the same as a PAT attempt, except that the kicking team must cover the kick in case it is missed, and the defending team attempts to run the ball back. A runback on a missed field goal is a rare occurrence.

The defensive team will attempt to block a PAT or field-goal attempt. In addition, the defensive team must be sure to be in position to stop a fake-kick attempt (an exotic). One method of blocking a kick is to come from the side. The rushers take an angle that will keep them from roughing the holder. They hope to get both hands on the ball just after it leaves the ground. The other kick-blocking method is the middle block. The defensive linemen attempt to drive the offensive linemen back while the jumper takes three steps and leaps to block the kick. A good surge by the linemen will get the jumper closer to the kicker, allowing him to block the kick before reaching its highest trajectory.

When the defensive team has stopped the offensive team on third down well away from the goal line, the offensive team will punt the ball. Excellent punting and coverage of the punt will gain valuable field position. To net 40 yards or more is a fine performance. "Net" means the total yards the punt covers, then subtracting the yards the ball is returned. So a 50-yard punt returned 15 yards would be a 35-yard net punt.

One punt formation used is the tight punt. Important elements from a kicking team standpoint are a fine snap, quickness in getting rid of the ball, protecting the kicker and covering to stop a return.

The punt formation used by most colleges and all professional teams is the spread punt formation. The advantage of this configuration is that the two wide receivers can potentially get down field quicker than their counterparts in the tight punt formation. In an NFL game, no one can cover the kick except for the two wide ends until the ball is kicked. With the ends split out, however, there is less protection for the punter.

NFL teams, as well as many college teams, normally try to double team the ends. The covering team in the NFL can not release any players (other than the ends) until the ball has been punted.

The return team has at least three strategies to use. The first is an attempt to block the kick. Overloading a side with a number of rushers is a possible strategy, as well as coming straight up the middle.

A second strategy is to use a side punt return. The front line attacks the punting team and then peels off forming a wall. The return man attempts to get behind the blockers in hopes of a substantial gain.

The third return strategy is to return the ball straight up the middle. If the covering team fans out exceptionally wide, this return can be most effective.

The defensive team attempts to ride the covering men toward the outside. Sometimes a crossblocking maneuver is also included to open a running lane for the return man.

On rare occasions, the offensive team could choose to quick kick on third down. A standard quick kick calls for the quarterback to pitch the ball to the halfback, who would kick the ball while moving laterally. The wide receivers would sprint down the field, downing the kick, thereby preventing a return.

Quick kicks were used frequently in the 1930s, '40s and '50s. After that time, it was an uncommon practice. The advantage of a quick kick is that there would seldom be any return, and often the kicking team would gain well over 40 yards in field position. If the defense was exceptional and/or the weather was poor, it was a sound strategy. The disadvantage would be that a chance to make a first down would be lost by surrendering the ball. Also, if the protection broke down, the kick might be blocked, since the kicker is much closer to the line of scrimmage.

The kicking game is one of the most important phases of football. A fourth of a team's video tape involves the kicking game. All close football games are decided by some kicking factor. The kickoff, punt return, field goal and extra point block, and blocked punt can work as an offensive weapon for the defense. It may become the determining factor between victory and defeat.

The main ingredient of a successful kicking game is execution. There are a number of important points to remember in the kicking game:

1. Do not move offside
2. Do not block below the waist
3. Do not rough the kicker
4. Do not illegally block on the punt return
5. Make sure to tackle the return man
6. Advance any kick blocked behind the line of scrimmage
7. Avoid very short kicks and partially blocked kicks that cross the line of scrimmage
8. Block a kick by going for the designated spot in front of the kicker
9. Always be alert for the unexpected: fake kicks and huddle alignments

The final key to the kicking game is effort. A team with great effort will have a good kicking game. To win defensively a team must not only stop the running and passing games, but must also win the kicking game.

I THINK HE WANTS TO BE TAKEN OFF THE KICK-BLOCKING UNIT...
MNRGF!
99

CHAPTER 10

Exotics: Adding a Dash of Spice

Trick plays (or "exotics") spice up many football games. Often an exotic might be one of the key plays in a ballgame. During the years that football has been played, trick plays have often sparked rule changes because they were so successful. Although the plays fell within the framework of the rules, they were almost impossible to stop.

For example, Paul "Bear" Bryant had a team at Alabama whose leading receiver was the left tackle. The rules stated that the end man on the line of scrimmage was eligible to receive a pass. It was impossible for the defense to tell if the tackle was eligible because the wide receiver would be split very wide and off the line of scrimmage. On the opposite side of the formation, the wide receiver would be up on the line of scrimmage. Again the defense could not tell who was eligible.

The rule now requires that not only must a player be on the end of the line of scrimmage, but also must have an eligible jersey number (1-49, 80-99). Another example of an unfair play was for an offensive team to have a receiver stand with his teammates on the sideline. At the last instant he would step onto the field. The ball would be snapped and the receiver would run down the sideline wide open to catch a pass for a big gain or a touchdown.

The new rules require that all men on offense must exit the huddle to legally be a part of the play. This eliminates any unfair type of play from the game. In addition, all players must stay in the "team area" which is six feet from the sideline.

Another example of an outlawed play was Nebraska's "fumblerooski." It is probable that the ball was not always fumbled but helped to the ground by the center. The backfield would run a play to one side, while the guard picked up the ball and ran in the other direction.

One of the simplest tricks is for the quarterback to change his voice inflection, emphasizing one word in an effort to convince the defense that the ball is going to be snapped so the defense will jump offsides, thus giving the offense five free yards with the ensuing penalty. "Drawing" or "pulling" the defense offside is most common on fourth down with less than five yards. To draw the defense offside, the quarterback would say, "Down, set, hut, hut, HUT! hut." Often, defensive players listen to the quarterback's voice instead of watching the ball.

The quarterback must be careful when he "barks" the loud sound that he does not "bob" his head. Motion, other than the standard sending of a back or receiver in motion, results in a penalty for falsely simulating the start of a play. If a quarterback does that, the official can, and should, penalize the offense.

When a coach finds his team near midfield on a fourth down and less than five yards to go, the (freeze) play is often called. The quarterback will sound the cadence and may change his voice inflection with no intent on having the ball snapped. The offensive team can take a delay of game penalty, followed by a punt and still have a fine opportunity to pin the opponent deep in his end of the field. Of course, if the defense gets impatient and jumps offsides the first down is gained.

A variation of the freeze is to have the ends shift during the cadence to get the opponent to jump offside. Again, if unsuccessful, they can take the delay of game penalty and punt the ball.

A third variation of the freeze is to have the quarterback go in motion while "barking" out the cadence. Again, the hope is to cause the defense to jump offside. I have even seen the ball snapped directly to the I-back and a scrimmage play attempted.

Just about every game includes one or more "reverses," usually by both teams. The play starts in one direction with the ball being pitched or handed to a teammate heading in the opposite direction. Defensive teams with a history of great pursuit are sometimes susceptible to reverses.

Fake reverse plays also can be very successful if the defensive team does not honor the original play. In the 1985 Nebraska vs. Oklahoma game played in Norman, Oklahoma, the leading rusher in the game for either team was a tight end, Keith Jackson. His gains were on three reverses gaining a total of 136 yards in Oklahoma's win. Keith had a long career in the National Football League and was a prominent member of the Green Bay Packers World Championship team of 1997.

Off of a reverse action, the ball can be pitched back to the quarterback, who in turn can throw a forward pass down the field. The hope is that the defense reacts to the reverse action and "goes to sleep" defending the pass. Also, the wide receiver can throw a pass. Diagram 10-1

Another "pitch back" or "flea flicker" is run by the offensive backs attacking straight ahead with the ball carrier pitching the ball back to the quarterback. In turn, the quarterback throws the ball down the field to an open receiver.

Another exotic that has been used successfully is the "hook and lateral." A pass is thrown to a receiver downfield and then lateraled to a back. The objective is that the defensive player will converge on the receiver, leaving the back open.

The "Academy Award" or "double pass" is executed by the

quarterback bouncing a lateral to the flanker. He catches the bounce pass, pauses showing disgust and then throws the ball to a receiver. The intent is that the defense will assume the play is over, relax and thus be out of position to stop the pass play.

A strong running team has the opportunity to throw a halfback or I-back pass. The goal is that the defensive backs will forget their responsibility and pursue to make the tackle on the back, thus leaving the flanker open. To be most effective, the I-back should tuck the ball and run aggressively, until stopping and throwing the pass.

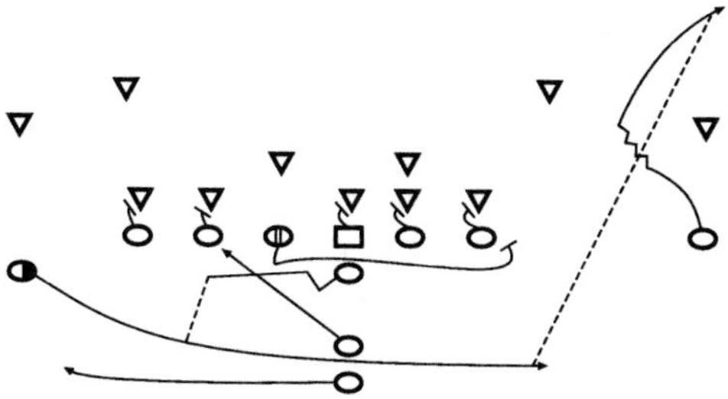

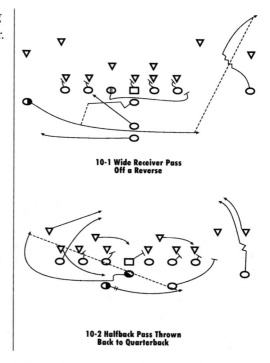

10-1 Wide Receiver Pass Off a Reverse

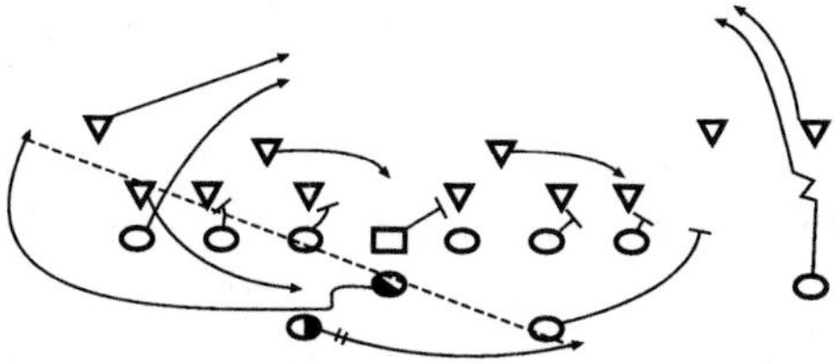

10-2 Halfback Pass Thrown Back to Quarterback

In the "red zone" (within 20 yards of the opponent's goal line) the halfback pass is sometimes thrown back to the quarterback. The red zone is shown in Diagram 10-2.

Really, there are six eligible receivers, not five with the sixth being the quarterback. The play is also used in other areas of the field.

Another effective pass play is for the quarterback to fake to a back, roll away, stop and throw back to that back. Again, the offensive team will hope that the defensive team forgets about the back.

Often, trick plays come in kicking game situations. In the old days, kickers used to kick straight ahead using their toes. However, that has changed. And since the "soccer-style" kicker is essentially the norm, especially in the NFL and major college football, the defensive teams tried to come up with ways to defend against their skills. The ability of soccer-style kickers to kick farther and more accurately prompted one very bizarre strategy. The strategy was for a tall defender to stand on the shoulders of another tall defender in hopes of blocking the kick. The rulemakers quickly deemed this strategy illegal due to the safety concerns for the defenders as well as to the "unfair" advantage of the maneuver.

In punting situations, teams line up in a punt formation and fake a punt, instead throwing a forward pass. If the defensive team does not cover the potential receivers, this type of play can be successful.

Another fake punt that has been successful is a direct snap to the fullback who runs off tackle with the help of trapping "up backs." An additional aid is for the punter to jump in the air and turn, simulating a high snap over his head. If even a few defenders are distracted, the play's chance for success increases.

A fake punt named after a former president and a colorful former coach has been very successful. On the West Coast it was named the "Tricky Dick," and the rest of the country knows it as the "Bummerooksi." The center snaps the ball directly to the fullback who steps forward, placing the ball between the upback's legs. The upback, with his arms crossed, receives the ball and stays hunched forward for two to three seconds (acting like he has a "tummy ache," is ideal). The fullback, after exchanging the ball, pivots and runs around the end. He is accompanied by the other upback and the punter. The fullback also yells, "reverse" to draw the defenders toward the flank. During this process, the linemen step inside and make themselves "big," desiring to shield the upback from the opponents. In the 1970s, UCLA set up a winning field goal with this play (6-3 final score), Stanford set up a score vs. Michigan in the 1972 Rose Bowl, and Nebraska scored a late first half touchdown vs. Missouri in 1975 to break open the game. Note: Fullback should "cheat" up to 4.5 yards, and the right upback should "cheat" back some.

Some successful fakes out of a PAT or field goal formation can be run. One successful run is the "shovel pass" to one of the wing backs. The ball is snapped to the holder, the kicker starts forward, and the ball is shoveled to a wingback coming behind the linemen.

A team may also try connecting a fake field goal pass or a two-point conversion pass from a hash mark closest to their bench. The end man on the line of scrimmage is pushed off towards the sideline by the next player toward the ball. The object is to make the defense believe that there are too many men on the field. As the guilty player runs toward his sideline, the ball is snapped to the holder, who raises up and throws a pass, often to a wide open receiver.

Another successful fake is to center the ball to the holder and send the wingback in motion across the formation. The holder gets up off his knee and rolls in the direction of the motion. Meanwhile, the "backside" tight end blocks half-heartedly, allowing the rusher to chase the holder. The holder then stops and throws the ball to the tight end, who is escorted by teammates toward the goal line. This is a "screen" pass from the PAT formation.

On PAT and field-goal attempts, many teams line up everyone but the center, holder and kicker off to the side. This allows the kicker and holder to get set exactly in position to attempt the kick. They then signal to their teammates to shift to a protection position. The PAT or field goal try is attempted after the shift.

However, if the defensive team ignores the bulk of the offensive team, they invite the "swinging gate" play to be attempted. The ball is snapped laterally to a back who runs behind blockers for a score. Also, the ball has been snapped to the kicker, and a pass is thrown. If the center has an eligible number, he is able to catch a pass because he is the end man on the line of scrimmage.

Even following a score, the receiving team must be alert for a possible onside kick. The kicking team might notice that the receiving team's front line retreats too quickly or there is a gap, allowing the "dribble kick" to be performed. The kickoff man approaches the ball, "dribble kicks" the ball to go 10 to 15 yards ahead, and in many cases recovers his own kick. If the play fails, however, the receiving team gains great field position.

The receiving team on the kickoff may attempt a reverse play that sometimes can be very effective if the covering team does not stay in their "lanes." However, because the ball is being run laterally, there is a chance to be tackled very deep in their own territory.

Another exotic sometimes used by the kickoff return team is the "throwback" pass play. The man receiving the kickoff will run to one side with some blockers, stop and throw back (lateral pass) to a teammate hanging back. Meanwhile, the front five men attack the cover men and then peel off forming a wall. The receiver of the pass runs behind the wall of blockers, often for a big gain.

Teams will not prepare to run this many exotics every game, but will have some similar plays ready to spring on the opponent. Successful plays add excitement to the game.

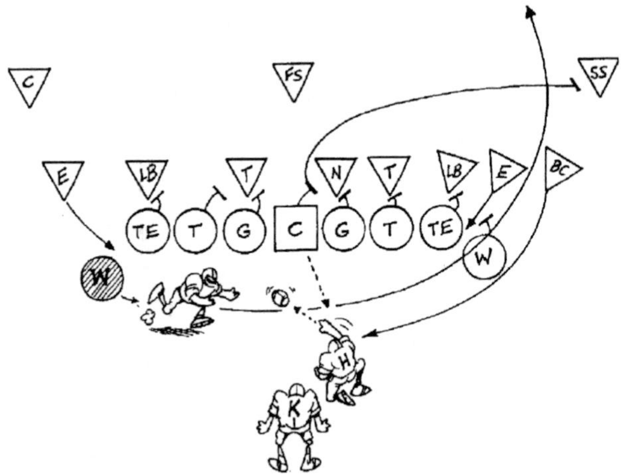

SHOVEL PASS

(OUT OF PAT OR FIELD GOAL)

Ball is snapped to holder. He catches it and "shovel passes" it to the left wing, who on the snap of the ball runs behind and parallel to the line of scrimmage. The block corner is allowed to rush clean while the other defenders are pinned to the inside.

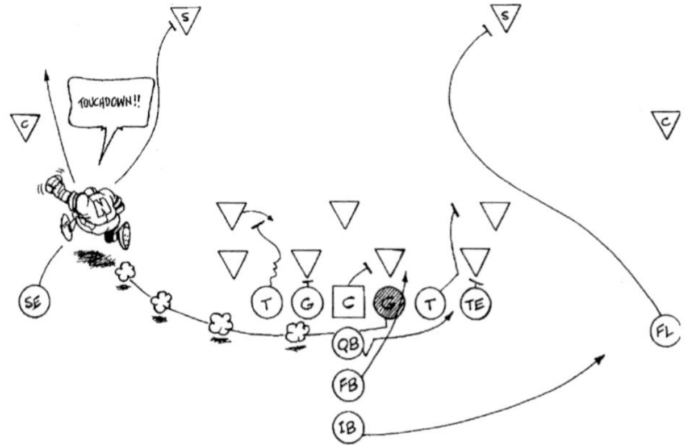

FUMBLEROOSKI

Ball is snapped to the quarterback who "fumbles" the ball with the center's "steadying" hand. Quarterback, fullback and I-back fake a dive option, going to the right. The right guard steps back, bends over, picking up the ball and runs to the left.

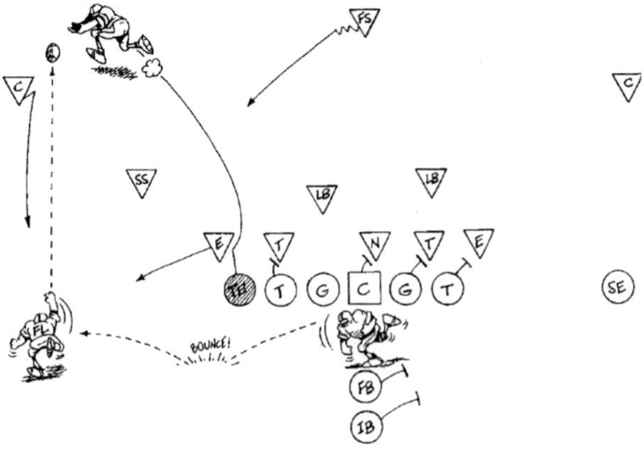

ACADEMY AWARD (BOUNCE PASS)

QB takes one step back and throws a bounce pass to the flanker. He catches the ball and physically shows disgust for an "apparent" incomplete pass while coming forth with appropriate expletives. The tight end, meanwhile, runs downfield, breaking behind the strong safety and corner. The flanker throws to the open tight end.

CHAPTER 11

Men in Polyester Shorts: (The Role of the Coach)

Often a coach serves as a substitute father to his players or as a father away from home. Obviously, some coaches become more involved in a player's personal life than others. Most, if not all, coaches are concerned about academic progress of a player, his behavior in school and off the practice field, and his effort and focus in meetings and practice.

Hopefully, a coach will serve as a positive role model for the athlete. Although college and professional coaches can have an effect on the athlete's development, it is generally assumed that a high school or junior high school coach has the greatest impact on the developing student-athlete.

Apart from the personal relationships with the players, the function of the coach is to prepare for meetings, practice and the game.

Organizing pre-practice meetings is very important. The better teacher the coach is, the more prepared his players will be to practice and play in the game. Printed material, the reviewing of tapes of the upcoming opponent, as well as verbal instruction are commonly used tools.

Preparation for the game starts very early in the week. Analyzing opponent's films, studying computerized data of their tendencies, focusing on how to negate the strengths of the opponent as well as plotting to attack their weaknesses dominate the agenda.

Some schools have offensive and defensive coordinators that do most of these tasks without asking for or accepting many suggestions from other assistants. Other programs, even with coordinators, are interested in every coach on the staff plotting the strategy. Give and take is freely asked for and expected.

Some head coaches are very involved in the planning and strategy for the upcoming game. Others delegate these tasks to coordinators and are more involved in administrative roles, public relations and dealing with the media.

The third element of preparation, once the plan is established, is to prepare cards and scripts to be used at practice.

Hours are spent drawing cards, scripting practice and

determining how much time to devote to each phase of the game at practice. Often coaches will work through lunch to finish all their tasks before player meetings (it may not look like many coaches miss meals, though).

During the season, the normal time expenditure of a college staff is to work 80 to 95 hours per week. Sunday meetings might start at 7 a.m. and last well into the night. Some of the staff may spend Fridays on the road scouting high school games. College coaches also have the added time constraint of making phone calls to prospective student-athletes during the week, a necessary additional duty for the program to succeed.

The coaching staff has to have a clear direction and focus. Likewise at any level, continuity of the coaching staff can be a key to success. High school players often pay attention to media reports about the lack of security for a particular coach's future. If a player signs a letter of intent to play for a school for the next four years, he is planning on playing for that particular coach for the full four years. However, schools can—and do—change coaches at the drop of a hat. That coach might bring in his own kind of players, leaving the recruits from the previous coach's tenure in a precarious position. Even if the players do stick around for the transition, the process itself can be emotionally taxing and stressful.

In more than 30 years, Nebraska has lost only one game to a team that had a losing record. That is even more impressive than winning the national championship. That is because Coach Bob Devaney and his successor, Tom Osborne, made sure the whole focus was on getting better every week—improvement. There are games that we have won on the scoreboard, but we treated them more like losses because we did not improve. Conversely, there are games we lost where we felt good because we made improvement, and that is what winning is to us. We can't berate our players for losing on the scoreboard if they have improved and played as well as they could. The approach is always to be a little better this week than we were last week.

CHAPTER 12

Practice, Practice, Practice

Normally, preparation leading up to the first game and then subsequent games starts with pre-practice condition drills. The drills may be organized and run by coaches, trainers or strength coaches, or simply by the individual athlete following a prescribed program.

Emphasis for these activities came to the forefront when some players died from heat stroke related maladies a number of years ago. These tragedies, along with the advice of doctors, prompted coaches and administrators at all levels to recognize that new attitudes and approaches must be taken.

The "official" practice procedure begins with fall camp (summer camp for the NFL). The general attitude of all involved in this experience is that it's a necessary evil. Generally, this time is often referred to as "Hell Week."

Often, teams will go to a site away from the school or NFL city. The prevalent idea is to go to an environment where all the focus is

on becoming a better player and a better team with minimal distractions (girlfriends, wives, friends, relatives, etc.).

Although practice and meeting times will vary, generally teams will practice at least twice a day for one-and-a-half to two hours with classroom meeting time scheduled in between practices.

Often one practice will be in T-shirts, headgear and shorts, or in shoulder pads, headgear, and shorts (half pads). The other practice often would be in full gear. The full pad practice may be in the morning to avoid the extreme heat of the afternoon.

Some coaches will add a third practice in the evening, often focused on the kicking game. Thus, the evening meeting would be shortened in the classroom or a third practice could simply be a "walk through" of points of emphasis that may include elements of not only the kicking game, but also of defense and offense.

Training camps generally involve three excellent meals a day with an evening snack, a lot of physical practice, as well as video tape viewing, coaches' lectures and reading of the playbook. There is little free time, and curfews normally are in force.

The goal of training camp is for the individual to approach his potential, to mold the individuals into a team, and to prepare the team for the first game and the season.

Coaches have learned that players do not all learn in the same ways. Therefore, various approaches are taken to educate the player about his responsibilities.

Generally, all players learn from the physical repetition of movements. However, some players cannot visualize their responsibilities from reading a playbook. Others do not have a clue as to what the coach is diagramming on a grease board, nor can they follow what the coach is saying.

Others gain little from watching a video, even of themselves, while some don't gain a great deal from a walk-through on the field, other than mere fresh air.

Once training camp is broken the team gets into a weekly game routine. There are five days of practice with different lengths and intensity, a game day and a rest day.

Although there are some differences, most teams give the players a day off following the game. Unless a player has been banged up, he would not come to the school or office on a day off.

This player day off allows the coaches to grade each player on each play of the previous game and then begin preparing for the next opponent. High school teams that play on Friday night might watch the video tapes of their team on Saturday morning, and then take Sunday off.

Monday's procedure for the players would be to have a team meeting to view the previous game, get new material with emphasis on the next opponent, and practice on the field. Often, a detailed scouting report is required.

Some coaches practice the players in half pads on Monday with greater emphasis being placed on all phases of the kicking game. There would be some practicing of offensive plays and defensive adjustments along with individual drills and technique work.

Other coaches would simply have a standard routine: individual drills, small group activities, and emphasis on offense, defense and kicking with some conditioning following the practice. Monday's practice generally is shorter than Tuesday and Wednesday's practices, which most coaches view as heavy work days.

Tuesday and Wednesday's practice procedure would begin with team and segment meetings. Following would be practice on the field beginning with stretching and warm-up activities, then small group and individual work, ending with team activities which would include some phases of the kicking game.

Conditioning activities would be done after practice. Also, during the week "maintenance" weight training activities are required. The goal is to keep players at the same strength level that they were in the summer.

Thursday's practice on the field normally would be shorter than the previous two days, but still include pre-practice meetings. Often situation segments would be included in this practice, specifically work in the red zone, two-minute drills simulating the end of the half or game, and various specific down-and-distance situations. Some teams would continue to practice in full pads while others might practice in sweat clothes. Friday's practice (if there is one) generally would be a half hour in length with loosening activities and a few selected plays practiced. In addition, some review of kicking is done. More time would be spent in classroom activities than on the field. Some teams, especially when playing an away game, might forego the Friday practice on the field.

Colleges are limited to 20 hours of player preparation per week. This includes a three-hour segment for the actual game. Increments of practice are very well defined. Often a manager will be assigned to do nothing but sound a whistle or horn, signifying the end of a period to keep everyone on schedule. Some schools will also flip cards at five-minute intervals so coaches can see where they are in practice. Creative uses of meeting time, video and actual practice procedure on the field are so important for a team to be properly prepared. The better a coaching staff can teach, the more prepared the team will be at game time.

Sample practice procedures for fall camp and for a regular week's practice are included in Diagram 12-1A and 12-1B.

Team DEFENSE (FULL PADS) Date 8/21/97

	NELSON	GEORGE	JON	CRAIG	CHARLIE
Meet					
3:00	STRETCH	STRETCH	STRETCH	STRETCH	STRETCH
3:05 Spec G R O U P	Warm-up Agil Tackle Rush vs. TE Pass Rush Speed Bull	Gold Cone Tackling Fumble Recovery Cut Drills		Cuts Tackle I'm Here Drops	Warm-up Agil.-FW Base Reach (AW) <u>Pass Rush</u> Shadow DT/Swim <u>Review</u> Mid, Open Wh, Blk
3:20		1 on 1	1 on 1	1 on 1 (Mike) (Rush)	
3:25	Skeleton 7 on 8 --->				
3:45	Full Team Skeleton--->				
3:50	Break--->				
4:00	Blitzes--->				
	Kicking--->				

TEAMWORK

Run Def.	Pass Def.	Run Off.	Pass Off.
3:15 2 - 1 3:32 1 - 2 Run & Stretch	Post Practice 1 C 2 Flat 1 P 2 Wh 3 Flat 10 2 Hk	1 - 2 2 - 1	

12-1A

Team Defense | Date 10/15/97

	NELSON	GEORGE	JON	CRAIG	CHARLIE
Meet					
3:00	STRETCH	STRETCH	STRETCH	STRETCH	STRETCH
3:05 Spec	Warm-up 5 Tech Pow G Option Boot	Blue Cut Drills Open Field Tackling		Hands Ct Reads Tackling Drill	Warm-up Agil.-FW Ev/Ov (G) (Onside Fold) Backside G)
G R O U P		ALL Corners 9 TechFS0/Rv 11 Rob Beating Stalk			
		Corners O/M 3 1 Qk Out 5 1 Out 5 1 P & C	Rv/FS 0/M vs. #2's 2 Slant 2 Out 2 Corner		3:50 Pass 1 on 1
	3:50 Pass 1 on 1				
3:20					
3:25	Skeleton 7 on 8--->				
3:45	Blitzes--->				
3:50	Break--->				
4:00					

TEAMWORK

Run Def.	Pass Def.	Run Off.	Pass Off.
4:25 GL & ShortYardage 4:38 Teamwork 4:50 Travel		Banjo Corners 1 & 2 Cross 1 & 2 Unders 1 TO 2 Deep Out	
4:55 1 - 1 5:05 Goal Line 1 - 1 5:10 Kicking 5:20 Stretch, Lift	2 - 2 2 - 2		

12-1B

CHAPTER 13

Squats, Curls, Gassers, and Carbs:

(The Role of Conditioning)

The development of players' bodies in the off season, as well as preparing them for practice and games, is vital. Much goes into the preparation of football players before the athlete ever practices or plays in a game. The appendix contains a sample pre/post-practice stretching program.

The first thing to do before and after a practice is to stretch the athlete to minimize the chance of injury. Prior to practice, the athlete stretches to warm the muscles; post-practice stretching rids the body of lactic acid. In addition to pre-practice stretching, coaches will have their players run and jog to prepare them for physical exertion.

Before an athlete even steps on the field, some schools, such as the University of Nebraska, use a fulltime nutritionist to educate him as to proper diet to allow for maximum physical development. The goal for each athlete is to reach the ideal ratio of body fat to lean muscle mass to perform at maximum efficiency. Understanding which foods will allow for the quickest achievement of the goal is desired. In addition, the long-term health benefits are noted. A strategy of accompanying the athlete on food shopping ventures has proven to be very effective in educating the athlete to the value of each food.

Recently, there has been emphasis on increased hydration. Greatly increasing amounts of water and other fluids has proven to add to the health of the athlete. Obviously, in warm climates fluid intake should increase to make up for losses during exertion. However, regardless of the weather, drinking large amounts of water has proven to be advantageous to the health of the athlete.

It is comical to see football players, many quite large, walking around with liter bottles of water—looking like "Baby Huey" nursing his bottle, yet it is encouraged, and in fact necessary, to keep the athlete as healthy as possible.

All college and professional teams and most high school teams have a strength program for their athletes. Generally, the program has a two-pronged approach. On one hand, in the off-season great emphasis is placed upon improving physical strength. Steady gains in strength is the goal.

The second approach is to maintain strength gained from the off-season during the competitive months. Instead of working 1 to 2 hours a day four times a week to develop strength, the regular season program generally requires 10 to 15 minutes of strength exercises four days a week. The purpose for maintaining strength, besides consistency of performance, is to decrease the number and severity of injuries.

Weight programs generally are divided between those who use machines to develop strength and those whose emphasis is on using free weights with proper spotting. Using machines allows for a safer environment and fewer injuries. However, the free weight proponents would point to greater development in auxiliary muscles for improved balance while getting stronger.

Another division of emphasis in weight training is between those coaches who believe in slow movements, fewer repetitions and very heavy poundage and those who emphasize explosive movement of the weight with less poundage and more repetition.

Coupled with a solid weight program are drills to improve the speed, quickness and agility of the football player, regardless of position. The off-season is the time when most of the emphasis is directed to making the athlete bigger, stronger and faster.

As the player gets closer to spring practice or the start of fall camp, the additional component of stamina and cardiovascular efficiency must be addressed. Some coaches ask their players to run continuously for set periods of time (distance running) to develop stamina. Others will ask players to run shorter distances with more repetition to develop the stamina to practice efficiently. One standard short burst program is to have players run back and forth across the field two complete times per set (gassers) in a prescribed

time period. Still others will simply have players dash or stride a set of 100-yard runs with little rest in between.

If a stadium is available, most coaches will have athletes run "stadium steps." Running to the top of many stadiums three or four times and walking down will quickly aid in getting the athlete in shape.

Increased athleticism includes higher stamina, improved speed, more quickness, better change of direction and increased strength. Results gained in off-season work normally translate into more wins during the season.

The psychological approach to the development of a player or team has always been important. Various approaches are used during a season. Getting athletes to "Win One for the Gipper" is on the extreme of getting players to play as hard as humanly possible. Avenging a last-season loss, responding to disrespectful statements from an opponent, or simply being focused to achieve a set goals are some of the motivations to get consistently great efforts from players. Teamwork, unity of purpose and sacrificing personal glory are themes that good programs incorporate. Teams with few selfish players tend to be most successful.

Many colleges use sports psychologists to aid the athlete in improving positive attributes and modifying negative traits. Audio and visual tapes as well as one-on-one meetings are often used. Getting a team to believe in itself is a key to winning.

CHAPTER 14

Men in Stripes: (The Role of the Official)

Everyone associated with a game should be pleased with a well-officiated contest. Officials performing their duties in a competent and professional manner aid in the play and enjoyment of the game. Do officials sometimes make mistakes? Yes, of course! But so do coaches and players.

The great majority of officials strive to do a competent job. A consistently incompetent official will soon become a "fan in the stands" and a dishonest official soon will be discredited. In all my years of playing and coaching football, I have seldom seen an obviously dishonest official. The few exceptions are a sad commentary on human nature.

An officiating crew must consist of at least four officials, each with specific duties. Additional officials can be added to make for a crew of up to seven.

It is advisable for officials to have worked together as a crew. A group of officials who make up a crew will do a better job than four to seven men who haven't worked together before.

Split crews used to be the norm on the collegiate level. A crew was made up of four officials from one conference and three officials from the other conference. The purpose was to have each team represented, but the statement, "That was one of your officials," in response to a complaint did not promote the image of an unbiased game.

I ASKED THE REF IF HE WAS BLIND OR SOMETHIN', AND HIS SEEING-EYE DOG ATTACKED ME...!

According to the *1996 NCAA Read-Easy Football Rules* some of the duties of the officials are as follows:

"THE REFEREE. The referee has general oversight and control of the game and is the sole authority of the proper score. His decisions upon rules and other matters pertaining to the game are final. The referee also administers penalties, making sure that both captains understand the procedure and outcome, and he inspects the field for any irregularities to report to game management. The initial position of the referee on scrimmage plays is behind and to the side of the offensive backfield where he observes shifts, legality of blocking, and play behind the neutral zone involving the ball. The referee is positioned in the area of the deep receivers or with the kicker on free kicks."

"THE UMPIRE. The umpire has jurisdiction over player equipment. He also is responsible for line play on both sides of the neutral zone. The umpire also is responsible for reminding the referee of the time remaining in each period. The initial position of the umpire on scrimmage plays is five to seven yards beyond the neutral zone where he adjusts his position to prevent interference with player movement. The umpire's position on free kicks is with the kicker or on the restraining line of the kicking team."

Many coaches feel there is no good place for the umpire to stand. At times he gets hit, often quite hard. The umpire sometimes deserves combat pay.

"LINESMAN. The linesman is responsible for the operation of the line-to-gain and down indicators. He instructs a line-to-gain crew, which consists of a minimum of two assistants and a third person who operates the down indicator. The linesman has jurisdiction over the neutral zone and infractions of the scrimmage formation, and he is responsible for indicating forward progress to the referee or umpire and for keeping track of the number of downs. On scrimmage plays, the linesman's initial position is in the neutral zone opposite the pressbox and wide enough to avoid interference with player movement. On free kicks, the linesman's position is at the receiving team's restraining line or at the 10-yard line opposite the pressbox."

"LINE JUDGE. The line judge has jurisdiction over the neutral zone and infractions of the scrimmage formation. As a member of a four-man crew, the line judge is responsible for timing the game, supervising the game-clock operator and ball persons, and counting defensive players.

The line judge indicates forward progress to the umpire and referee. On scrimmage plays, the initial position of the line judge is in the neutral zone on the pressbox side of the field and wide enough not to interfere with player movement. As a member of a four- or five-man crew, the line judge is positioned at the 10-yard line of the receiving team. In a seven-man crew, the line judge is positioned on the sideline."

"BACK JUDGE. The responsibilities of the back judge include counting defensive players, timing the game, ruling on long passes and kicks, and the status of the ball in his area. The back judge observes eligible receivers leaving the neutral zone. On scrimmage plays, the back judge in a five-, six- or seven-man crew is positioned approximately 20 to 25 yards beyond the neutral zone and deeper than the defensive backfield. The lateral position is determined by the use of a field judge or side judge. On free kicks, the back judge in a five-, six- or seven-man crew is at the sideline at the 10-yard line of the receiving team."

"FIELD JUDGE. The field judge is responsible for timing the 25-second count and observing eligible receivers, kicks and passes on his side of the field. On scrimmage plays, the field judge in a six- or seven-man crew is positioned approximately 15 to 20 years deep on the defensive side of the neutral zone on the side of the field opposite the pressbox and wide enough to avoid interference with player movement. On free kicks, the field judge in a six- or seven-man crew is at the 10-yard line on the linesman's sideline."

"SIDE JUDGE. The side judge is responsible for observing eligible receivers, kicks and passes on his side of the field. During scrimmage plays as a member of a seven-man crew, the side judge is positioned approximately 15 yards behind the defensive side of the neutral zone on the pressbox side of the field and wide enough to avoid interference with player movement. On free kicks, the side judge is positioned on the sideline at the receiving team's restraining line."

Diagram 14-1 shows the positioning of the officials in a seven-man crew on a scrimmage play.

Also, the official's signals for penalties including holding, clipping, illegal block, offsides, illegal motion, false start, facemasking, tripping, too many men on the field and delay of game—as well as short definitions of each penalty—are shown in the appendix.

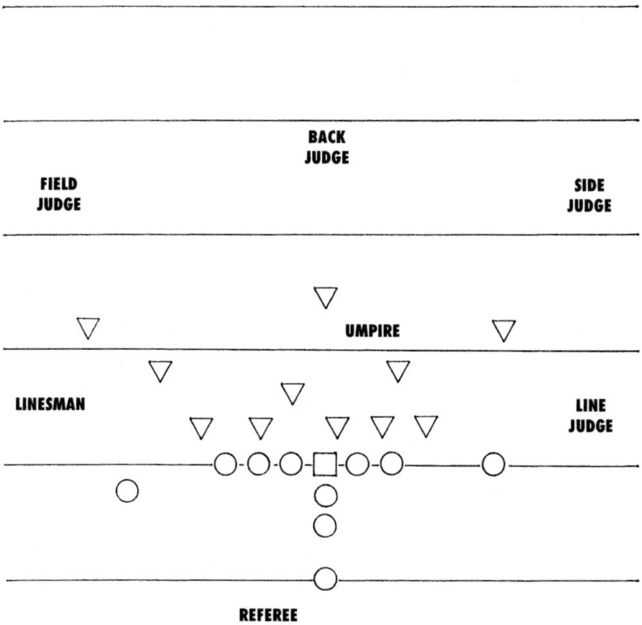

DIAGRAM 14-1 POSITION OF OFFICIALS

CHAPTER 15

Pulling it All Together: Game Day

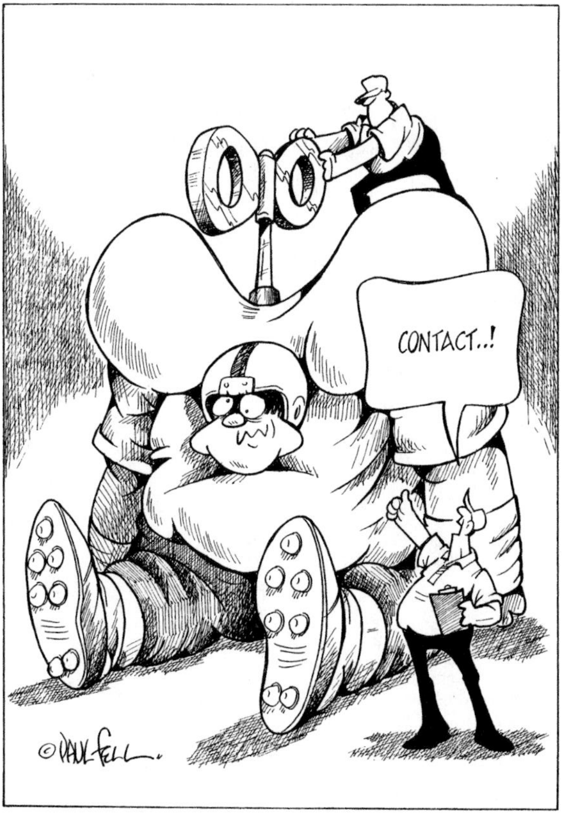

At the game, coaches in the press box and on the sideline have their game plan. Every possibility is anticipated. Communication between the pressbox and field flows continually. Teams must adjust to each other's tendencies in order to be successful.

Calling offensive and defensive plays and keeping them clear, as well as watching what the opponent is doing, is a continuing process.

Some offensive coaches will already have decided on a set number of plays to be run in succession before the game starts. Usually, these plays are run out of various formations to see how the opponent is adjusting. In addition, the first play may be designed with the hopes of getting a big gain to get the defense back on their "heels."

The great professional coach Vince Lombardi was purported to often call for the first play or two to be directed at the best defenders. He desired to get excellent blocks on their best players. Hopefully, with success against the best defenders, the defense would start to lose confidence.

Conversely, the defensive coaches may take a conservative approach at first, or blitz to obtain a big defensive play, getting the offense off to a bad start. Regardless of the various approaches, much thought and planning has gone into preparing for the game by both staffs.

Sample game plans are found in Diagrams 15-A, 15-B, 15-C, 15-D and 15-E.

DOWN & DISTANCE - K-STATE

LONG YD (3rd 6+) (19% Blitz)

S.G.
34 QB Draw ✔
32 Flush Pass ✔
71 2 Under
71 Aud
71 Dbl Del IB Drag
71 D.T.O.
42 S.P. Rt ✔
71 Dbl Del

Wide Rt
56 Draw
71 2 Out FB Flat Prot

Ace
71 JB Lt 1 Mot
31 Spnt ✔

Spd Rt
34 IB Draw
71 2 Opt Pass
SG 79 IB ✔ Prot

Pro Rt
79 9 P & C FB Flat Prot

MEDIUM LONG YD (3rd 3, 4, 5) (6% Blitz)

Dbl Wing
11 Wall ✔
71 Aud

Pro Rt
32 Opt Seal SM
34 QB Keep
F 42 CS Boot Lt Stop Fl Mot
43 Dive P FB Del Flat
F 42 CS Boot Lt 9 Del Fl Mot

Ace
31 Spnt ✔ (1 Mot)
71 JB Lt 1 Mot

Wide Rt
41 Spnt ✔
32 Opt ✔
11 Base Solid

SG
31 Spnt ✔
34 QB Draw
42 S.P.
71 Dbl Del IB Drag

Tight Rt
11 B ✔
F 42 CS Boot Lt TE Deep SM

Power Rt
41 Spnt

Open Rt
49 Spnt Crack

SHORT YD (3rd, 4th, 2 or less) (0% Blitz)

Power Rt
44 Iso
48 Power WBM
11 Base
41 O.S.
32 Opt
14 S

Tight Rt
44 Iso
48 Power (Fl Mot)
11 Base
41 P
32 Opt
Near 44 Iso P 2 Up

Ace
31 Spnt ✔
42 CT ✔

LONG YARDAGE GL (1st 7+, 2nd 5+, 3rd 3+ inside 10)

Power Rt
41 Spnt ✔
11 B ✔
32 Opt
48 Power Pass WBM
F 48 CS Boot Rt GL WBM

Pro Rt
99 Fade

Ace
31 Spnt

SG
34 QB Draw
42 S.P. Rt

BIG PLAYS

Power Rt
19 Opt P WB Flag SM Prot
F 48 CS Boot Rt TB SM
49 OS Pass IB Deep SM

Tight Rt
.1 Opt P 1 Slnt & Go TB Prot

Spd Rt
47 Draw P F Rev Fl Mot Prot

SG
71 DTO

Ace
43 Draw P D.T.O.
42 CS 1 Rev Lt
42 CS F Rev

Dbl Wing
11 Opt P 2 Deep

Wide Rt
11 Opt P 1 Hook & Go Prot
43 Draw P WB Seam IB Mot Prot

Pro Rt
F 42 CS Boot Lt Wheel Fl Mot
19 Opt P 9 Slnt & Corner Prot

15-A

VIRGINIA TECH - 1996

2 BACKS 1 TE

Fronts	Stunts	Cov.
Even (Stg)	Screw, Stab, Go	11R, 4, 9
Ov (Stg)	Jet, Veer	Bracket
*Even Whip	Screw,	0
Bubble Ov (Stg)		
Bubble Under	Tiger, Stab	0
Fire Blitz		
Single/Double	Switch	1 Zip
Bubble Mike	Go, Switch, Stab, Nose, Tackle	1 Zip
Bubble Ov Wanda	Stab, Twist	Zorro Wk
*(Split Backs) If alot of Split Backs		
Zone Blitz		
Even Gut	Cross	9 Gut
Man Blitz		
*Sub Blitz (X)		11 Sub (X)
*Rambo		1 Peel
Black		2 Blac

2 BACKS 2 TE

Fronts	Stunts	Cov.
Even (Stg)		Go Screw 11R, 4
Ov Stg		Go Screw 11R, 4
Bubble Ov/Und		0
Fire Blitz		
Single Switch		1 Zip
Bubble Mike		1 Zip
Man Blitz		
Sub		11 Sub
Black		2 Black
Short Yardage		
Short Single Snk Double (Screw) Bolt Short		1 Free
Doubles Psycho Hard Lock		

2 Backs 3 Wide

Even (Stg)	Stab, Go	11R, Bracket, 4, 9
Ov (Stg)	Jet, Veer	
Even Whip		0
Bubble Ov		0
Bubble Und	Tiger	0
Fire Blitz		
Single/Double	Switch	1 Zip
Bubble Mike	Go, Switch, Stab, Nose, Tackle	1 Zip
Bubble Ov Wanda	Stab, Twist	Zorro Wk
Zone Blitz		
Even Gut	Cross	9 Gut
Man Blitz		
*Sub Blitz (X)		11 Sub
*Rambo		1 Peel
Black		2 Black

1 Back 3 Wides

Fronts	Stunts	Cov
Even Stg	Screw Stab Go	11R, Bracket, 4 9
Ov Stg	Screw Stab Go	
Even Whip		0
Bubble Ov		0
Bubble Und	Tiger	0
Fire Blitz		
Single/Double		1 Zip
Bubble Mike		1 Zip
*Bubble Ov Wanda	D. Stab, Twist	Zorro Wk
*Bubble Und Wanda	D. Stab, Twist	Zorro Wk
Zone Blitz		
*Ov Fire	Stg Sting Mike Shoot	Viking Stg
*Even Gut	Cross	9 Gut
Man Blitz		
Rambo		1 Peel
Black		2 Black
Sub (X)		11 Sub (X)

ACE

Fronts	Stunts	Cov.
(Hash) Even Stg	Go Screw	11 R, 4 Pl
Bubble Ov/Und		Bracket
		0
Fire Blitz		
Single/Double		1 Zip
Bubble Mike		1 Zip
Zone Blitz		
Ov Fire	Stg Sting Mike Shoot	Viking Stg
Man Blitz		
Black		2 Black
Sub		11 Sub

1 Back 4 Wides

Even	Go	11R, Bracket, 4 Live, Pl, 9 Live, PP
Fire Blitz		
Single/Double	Switch	1 Zip
Bubble Mike	Stab	1 Zip
Bubble Und/Ov	Wanda, Dbl Stab, Twist	Zorro Stg
Zone Blitz		
Ov Fire	Sting Mike, Shoot	Vik St
Even Gut	Cross	9 Gut
Man Blitz		
Rambo		1 Peel
Black		2 Black
Sub		11 Sub
Black		2 Black

15-B

Short Yardage

	Cov.
Short Single Snk Double (Screw) Short Doubles Psycho Hard Lock	1 Free

Goaline

Red Zone

Even (Stg)	Panther
Single/Double	1 Zip
Bubble Mike	1 Zip
Black	2 Black
Rambo	1 Peel

2 Point

Even Stg	Zone

Hurry Up

Even Stg	11R

15-C

TE 81 40 　 QB 16 5 　 PUNT 95

SE 4 31 　 FB 44 (34) 　 PLK 17

(15) FL 22 48 　 TB 28 34 　 HOLD 91

SNAP 72

B

V. T.

BEHIND

	1-10	1-S (-4)	2-L (10-8)	2-M (7-4)	2-S (3-1)	3-L (10-5)	3-M (4-3)	3-S (2-1)	4-L (+3)	4-S (2-1)	1-XL	2-XL	3-XL	4-XL
+G TO +7	BUB UN-O (NAIL) BUB OV-O (NAIL) (49G PB10)		BUB OV-O BUB UN-O (14 SM)											
+8 TO +25	BUB UN-O BUB OV-O (NAIL/SCR) EV. WHIP SCREW-WO SINGLE BL-1ZIP PIT-2 DVOP | 150-4 SPLZ 5K | DDB-5 SBP DDK R-60% (★1SCR)		BUB UN.-O (JET) EV. STG (GO/JET) 11R 4PI ★BUB OV. WANDA DBTW ★RAMBO-1PEEL ZOR. WK (DDB-3/SDP-2) P-100%	EV. SUB BL.-11SUB EV. SUB BL X-X11SUB (11 DVOP)		OV. STG (GO/NOSE) BRACK-9P.I. ★RAMBO-1PEEL (DDB-2) P-100%						EV. STG (GO) BRK (DDB)	EV. STG GO-4PI-11R ★RAMBO 1PEEL (ADB/DDB) P-100%	
+26 TO +50	BUB OV/UN-O (NAIL/SCR) EV/OV. STG.-11R/4PI (STAB/GO) BUB OV. M SW-1ZIP BUB UN. M SW-1ZIP ★BLACK-2 BLK (DVOP | 150-8 SPLZ-3 DRZ DVF | SDP-2 DDK SSP SBP WHP) R-70% (★1SCR)		EV. STG-11R BUB UN-O ★ BUB OV. WANDA DBL STAB-ZOR. WK ★ OV. FIRE STING VIK. STG ★ OV FIRE M. SHOOT VIK. STG (DVOP | DRZ CB | DDB-2 SDP) P-60%	EV. STG (GO/STAB) 11R OV. STG (TAC) 11R BUB OV-O (NAIL) ★RAMBO-1PEEL (DVOP PIT CS | DDB-3 WPP SDP-2 DDK) P-70% (★1SCR)	BUB OV (SCR) O (37 DRZ CB)	EV. STG (GO/JET) BRACKET ★BUB OV. WANDA TWIST-ZOR. WK ★RAMBO-1PEEL ★ GUT-9GUT P.I. (41GPT | DDB-6) P-85%	EV. STG (GO/JET) BRACKET/9PI OV. STG (GO) BRK 9PI. ★ GUT-9GUT P.I. (DDB-2 ADB) P-100%	2) EV. WHIP SCR WO BUB UN (TG) O 1) SING. SNK (DBL SCR) 5 IFR (43150-2 47SPLZ) R-100% (2-45150 1-47SPLZ)				EV. STG (GO/STAB) 11R EV. WHIP SCR-WO (DVOP-2 PIT / DDB DDK) R-60% (★1SCR)	OV. STG (GO) 4PI/11R EV STG (GO) 4PI/11R ★ RAMBO 1PEEL (DDB-2) P-100%	
-50 TO -21	BUB OV-O (SCR) BUB UN-O (SCR) EV. STG (GO/STAB)-11R EV. WHIP SCR-WO SINGLE SW (WK)-1ZIP ★EV. SUB BL.-11SUB ★OV. SUB BLX-X11SUB (DVOP-2 PIT CS | 150-3 SPLZ DVF | DDB-2 SBP DDK-2) R-67% (★2SCR)		EV. STG (GO)-11ROB OV. STG (NOSE)-11ROB OV. SUB X-X11SUB EV. SUB BL (GO)-11SUB (DVOP | 1DB SOP WOP) (NO INSIDE RUN) P-75%	BUB UN-O BUB OV.-O (SCR) (49 DVOP/QDB) 50-50	EV. WHIP SCR O BUB UN-O SINGLE SW WK-1ZIP (150-2/SDP) R-67%	EV. STG (GO) 11R 49 DVOP | SDP DDK P-67% (★1SCR)		2) BUB OV-O 1) SING. SNK (DBL SCR) SH IFR (48POWG-2 49GTSNP) R-100%				BUB UN-O (NOSE) BUB OV-O (TAC) (DDB DDK) P-100% (★1SCR)	EV STG (GO/JET/ST) 11R OV. STG (TAC) 11R ★RAMBO-1PEEL (DDB-2) P-100%	
-20 TO -16	EV. STG (GO)-4PI OV. STG TAC-4PI (49GSNP/SSP-DDK) P-67% (★1SCR)		OV. BUB-O (36 TK)		OV. STG (SCR) 11R (48CS)	EV. STG GO-11R OV. STG TAC-11R P-100% (★1SCR)			EV. STG GO 11R ★ SUB BL.-11S (DDB)					
-15 TO -11			MAV → 4FF	BUB OV. M SW-1ZIP SING SW. WK-1ZIP (47150)										
-10 TO -6		BUB UN M-GO 1ZIP EV. STG (GO) PAN F R-100% (PITCHES)												
-5 TO -G	[redacted]	EV. STG (GO) ZONE DB. PSY-HARD LOCK (TK-150G) R-100% (INSIDE)	[redacted]	EV. STG (GO) ZONE DB. PSY-HARD LOCK (TK-150G) R-100% (INSIDE)	EV. STG (GO) ZONE DB. PSY-HD LOCK SMOKE-O R-100% (DVF/POWG)		EV. STG (GO)-ZONE DB. PSY-HARD LOCK R-67% (GP B10/47150/SPP)	DB. PSY-HARD LOCK SMOKE-O (47150)		DB. PSY HARD LOCK SMOKE-O (43150)				

15-D

TE 81 40	QB 16 5	PUNT 95	
SE 4 31	FB 44 (34)	PLK 17	
FL 22 48	TB 28 34	HOLD 91	
		SNAP 72	

A

AHEAD

	1-10	1-S (-9)	2-L (10-8)	2-M (7-4)	2-S (3-1)	3-L (10-5)	3-M (4-3)	3-S (2-1)	4-L (+3)	4-S (2-1)	1-XL	2-XL	3-XL	4-XL
+G TO +7														
V.T. +8 TO +25	BUB OV/UN-O (NAIL/SCREW) BUB OV/UN MIKE (SW)-1ZIP EV/OV (STG)-11R (PIT/150·DRZ/SCR) R-93% (★1 SCR)		EV. STG (STAB)-11R (41DVOP/37DRZ CB) R-100%	BUB OV-O (SCR/NAIL) BUB UN·O SING SW (WK)-1ZIP EV. STG (GO)-11R ★ BLACK-2 BLK (PIT-3 | DRZ·150 DVF | SDP) R-90%		EV. STG -11R (GO) (150/SDP) 50-50 (43150/SDP)		2) BUB OV-O (SCREW) (48POWG/48150) R-100%			EV. WHIP SCR-WO EV. STG 11R (37DRZ)		EV. STG (GO/JET) 11R (DDB)	
+26 TO +50	BUB UN/OV-O (SCREW/NAIL) EV. STG (STAB)-11R/4P.I. OV. STG (NOSE/TAC)-11R/4P.I. ★ OV.(STG) SUB BL.(GO) 11SUB ★ EV (STG) SUB BL (GO) 11SUB (PIT-6 POW-3 CS-1 | 150-16 TK-3 DV-2 | DDB-4 SDP-1 WPP-1) R-85%		① BUB UN/OV-O EV. STG SCR-WO EV. STG (SCR/GO) 11R SINGLE SW-1ZIP (DVOP-3 | 150-2 TK-2 SPLZ DRZ | DDB-4 SDP) R-60% (★1 SCR)	BUB UN/OV-O BUB UN M SW-1ZIP EV WHIP SCR-WO EV STG (STAB) 11R 4PI EV. SUB BL (X)-11S OV. SUB BL X-X11S (PIT-2 OS | 150-4) R-100%	BUB UN (STAB) O EV. STG (GO/STAB) 11R (PIT/SPLZ/DDB DDK) 50-50 (★1 SCR)	EV. STG (GO)-11R (SCR) BRACK. OV. STG GO-BRACK 11R ★BUB UND WANDA DBL STAB/JET ZOR. WK (CS | 150 | DDB-7 SRP DDK) P-82% (★1 SCR)	EV/OV. STG (GO) BRACKET PRESS ★BUB OV. WANDA DBL. (STAB/TWIST) ZOR. WK ★ RAMBO-1 PEEL ★ OV. FIRE M-SHOOT VIK STG P-75% (47150/3-DDB)	2) BUB OV. (SCR)-O 1) SH SING SNK-DBL BOLT/DBL SCR SH 1FR (3106)	BUB OV-O BUB OV SCR O 4/5(+35) (43150)		EV. STG STAB-11R OV. STG NOSE-11R BUB OV. M TAC-O (150DR/TK DDK) R-67% (★1 SCR)	EV. STG (STAB/GO) 11R/4PI (150/SRP DDB DDK) P-75% (★1 SCR)	OV. FIRE STING VIK STG OV. FIRE M-SHOOT VIK STG RAMBO-1 PEEL EV. STG GO BRK/9PI (DDB-4 SDP) P-100%	
-50 TO -21	BUB OV./UN-O (SCREW/NAIL TIGER) OV./EV. (STG) GO, STAB-11R, 4PI EV. STG SCREW-WO SINGLE SW-1ZIP BUB UN. M. SW-1ZIP (PIT-2 DVOP-2 CS-2 | 150-13 DRZ(CB)-6 DV-3 | DDB-8 WDP-2 DDK-1 SRK-1) R-68% (★2 SCR)		BUB UN-O (TIGER) EV. STG (GO/STAB) 11R 4PI. ★ BUB OV WANDA DBL STAB-ZWK ★ BUB UN. WANDA DBL STAB-ZWK (DVOP-2 | DV 150 TK | DDB SRP SDP) R-67%	BUB UN/OV-O (SCR) EV. WHIP SCR-WO EV. STG. (GO/STAB) 11ROB/4 P.I. CS-2/150-4/DDB-3 PIT DDK R-65% (★1 SCR)	BUB OV. SCR O BUB OV. M SW 1ZIP (42POW-2/150-2 DVF) R-100%	EV. STG (GO/JET) BRACK-11R ★RAMBO-1 PEEL OV. STG TAC-BRK 11R (DDB-8 WWP) P-100%	EV. STG (STAB) 11R EV. STG SCR 11R. 50-50 (42POWG/SRP)		EV. STG (GO) BRACK. 4/13(-30) (DDB)	1) SH SING SNK-DBL SCR. SH 1FR 4/1(-30) (145M)	EV. STG SCR-11R (43150)	EV. STG POW-11R RAMBO 1PEEL (PIT/DVOP | DDB 3) P-60% (A1-SHOVP)	EV. STG (JET) 11R/BRK OV. FIRE M-SHOOT VIK SRG RAMBO 1PEEL (DDB-4 DDK) P-100% (★1 SCR)	
-20 TO -16	BUB UN/OV-O (TIGER-SCR STAB) EV WHIP SCR-WO SINGLE SW (WK)-1ZIP (42POW | 150-2 TK SPLZ) R-100%		BUB OV-O EV. STG (GO)-9FPI. (DDB DDK) P-100% (★1 SCR)	SINGLE SW-1ZIP (34TK)	R-67% (★1 REV)	EV. STG (GO/STAB) OV. STG (NOSE) 4PI BRACK (DDB)	EV. STG (SCR) 11R OV. STG (GO) 11R BRACK 50-50 (36DVF/DDB)						SINGLE SW (WK) 1ZIP (16QBDR) 3/14(-19)	
-15 TO -11	EV. STG (GO) PAN F OV. STG (GO) PAN F (PIT REV | 150 | DDB-3) 50-50 (★1 REV ★1 SHOVP)		EV. STG (GO/STAB) PAN F OV. STG (NOSE) PAN F (DDK-2 WWP) P-100% (★2 SCR)	EV. STG GO-PAN F OV. STG (GO)-PAN F OV. SUB (GO)-11S (41 PITCH)		EV. STG (GO) PAN F 50-50 (47150/DDB)						EV/OV STG-PAN. (TAC/GO) (DDB) 2/13(-15)		
-10 TO -6	EV. STG (GO)-PAN F OV. STG (TAC) PAN F 1/10(-10) (DDB)	SING. SW-1ZIP OV. STG SCREW PAN F (48POWG 3105 | DVF DV 150) R-100%	EV. STG (SCREEN) PAN F (3 BACKS-√43 REV.) (34TK/48POWG) R-100%	EV. STG (SCR) PAN F OV. STG (GO) PAN F (48 POW — DDB SRP) P-67%		EV. STG ([illegible]) PAN F (I50 / SCR DDB WPP) P-75%								
-5 TO -G		DB. PSY-HARD LOCK SMOKE-O (POWG2) 150-SDP R-75%			DB. PSY-HARD LOCK 1/3(-5) 34DVF/[illegible] R-100%			DB. PSY-HARD LOCK SMOKE-O 3/3(-5) (42 POWG)		DB. PSY. HARD LOCK SMOKE-O 1/1(-1) (43150)				

CHAPTER 16

The Buyer is a Liar: The Joy of Recruiting

A late colleague used to say, "The buyer is a liar, until he signs." This simple axiom guides my recruiting. I don't take anything for granted until the letter-of-intent is signed.

Attracting players to be a part of a football team is extremely important for a team to be successful (and for more young men to learn lessons that will serve them well later in life).

A junior high school coach encouraging a young boy to try out for the team is often the key to the boy playing football for a number of years. In high school, some players will see the opportunity to get a scholarship to college due to their football skills coupled with their academic achievement.

A successful coach in secondary education will not only work with the teens who want to play football, but will also encourage the promising boy in gym class (or "walking the halls") to try out for the team. Sometimes those young men advance the furthest in the sport.

One of my pet peeves is to see coaches in various schools forcing a young man to choose only one sport in which to participate. Sometimes a student-athlete misses out on positive experiences, as well as scholarship opportunities, because of choosing the wrong sport! I firmly believe that allowing a young man to play as many sports as he desires is ideal. Skills developed in one sport often aid in success in another. Development of poise in stressful situations can be achieved.

Of course academic achievement must be evident to allow for participation in numerous extracurricular activities. Various studies have shown that athletes' grades are better during the season. Many states have rules governing participation depending on minimum grades.

College programs must attract outstanding student-athletes to have any hope of fielding winning teams. The reputation of the school, the past success of the football team, the impression made by coaches on the family, and the proximity of the school to the prospect's home are generally key factors in choosing a college to attend.

Because of the pressure on coaches to win or be fired, as well as natural competitiveness, rules were developed to establish a framework for college recruiting procedures. Scholarships to Division 1-A schools are exactly the same (room, board, books, tuition and fees are universal awards). The total number of scholarship players on each team is the same (unless previous recruiting violations have caused a temporary reduction in the total).

Each prospect can accept only a specific number of paid recruiting trips to colleges (in 1997, only five official visits were allowed). A head coach can visit a prospect and his family only one day during the recruiting season. Assistant coaches are limited to a weekly contact during the recruiting season.

A national letter-of-intent program is in place. On or after a certain date, a player and his family sign a contract committing to a particular school. The prospect is required to attend that school for at least one year after signing the letter.

Football rules in Division I-AA, Division II and Division III are tailored to allow for fair competition as much as possible. Fewer scholarships per team are awarded, or in the case of Division III, no athletic grants-in-aid are awarded.

Present rules do not allow for coaches to be with prospects on that magic day of signing (in fact, coaches can not be "off campus" the whole week). The following incidents could not happen today; they did in the past before this intelligent rule was passed.

A prominent quarterback recruit in California signed a national letter-of-intent to Stanford University. The papers were placed in the mail box. In the meantime, University of California coaches convinced the prospect's brother to have him change his mind. The prospect did change his mind, signed a second contract with California, and somehow the first letter was retrieved from the post office before it was sent.

Even before the letter-of-intent rules were instituted, coaches sometimes were not good role models. Following a Big 33 All-Star game in Hershey, Pennsylvania, between teams from Texas and Pennsylvania, two coaches from rival universities got into a fistfight over a recruit.

Many college coaches would arrive at a prospect's home at 8 a.m. on national letter-of-intent day only to find a coach or coaches from other schools also there, sitting in a living room making small talk as the prospect and parents are in and out of the kitchen or bedroom trying to make a decision on which scholarship to accept. This was not only stressful for the prospect and coaches, but in hindsight always seems rather comical.

A few highly creative coaches tried to lessen the stress of this type of situation. Many heavily recruited prospects during the years have suddenly disappeared from school a day or two prior to the day of intent. A university would hide the player out at an alumnus' house or a friendly high school coach's home to keep the "competition" away. On signing day, sometimes the parents and prospect would sign the contract away from the home to avoid pressure from other college coaches.

Unfortunately, a coach can only be at one house at a time. The University of Nebraska lost out signing three top prospects in the early '70s because the fine coach recruiting them was flying from one city to another while three other colleges had one coach assigned to each prospect.

Once I was recruiting a prospect in California who was deciding between Nebraska and a West Coast college. I visited his high school the morning before the signing date and was informed by the high school coach that the boy would contact me by noon with his decision. I went back to the motel and watched "inspiring" morning television until 11:30. Since I had not heard from the boy, I called the high school coach. He informed me that coaches from the prominent West Coast university had gotten the prospect's sister (who was home from school due to illness) to go to the principal of the high school reporting a serious situation at home. The request to excuse the prospect from school was approved, and the prospect was taken to an alumnus' home to be kept away from recruiters.

The high school coach said, "All bets are off. Do what you have to do to get the prospect." I immediately went to the prospect's home, was invited in by the prospect's mother and sat in the living room watching "inspiring" afternoon television. Later in the afternoon when the boy's father came home he asked me, "Where is my son?" My response was, "They kidnapped him!"

Obviously angry, he asked again. I again responded with the

same reply, further increasing his anger. Shortly after that exchange, the doorbell rang, and a well-dressed middle-aged gentleman was admitted. He said he came by to get clothes and toiletries for the prospect. The father said, "Where's my son?" The man said he did not know his whereabouts.

The father exploded and threatened to call the state police because the man obviously knew where the prospect was. He demanded in no uncertain terms that his son had better be returned in short order or the authorities were going to be called. Continuing to watch television and adding only a few inflammatory comments, I waited for the prospect to arrive.

The prospect arrived around suppertime. Shortly after that a guidance counselor (who was on my side) arrived, and everyone but the ill sister and me (the TV critic) went in a bedroom. I could hear some heated conversation through the door. Finally, the family and guidance counselor came out of the bedroom announcing that the prospect was coming to Nebraska. After hugs and handshakes, I left to get a late supper and a short night's sleep. Knowing the competition, I felt it was not yet over.

The next morning I arrived in front of the prospect's house at 6:30 a.m. Sure enough, about 7:15 a.m. a big Cadillac pulled up and

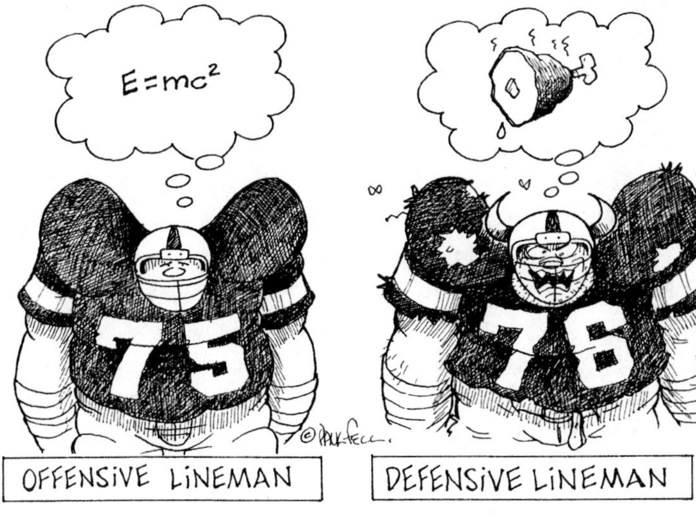

another well-dressed gentleman exited the car. We walked up to the porch shoulder to shoulder. I asked him what he was doing. He said he was coming to congratulate the prospect on choosing to attend the West Coast college. I informed him of his misinformation as we rang the doorbell. We were invited into the living room. To my pleasure the choice of Nebraska was reaffirmed, and I did not have to endure further examples of the "inspiring" day-time television.

The problem of alumni involvement has now been greatly reduced, since it is a violation for an "alum" to be a part of the recruiting process. I have no doubts that the visit by the alumnus would have involved an illegal inducement had I not been at the home. Overzealous alumni, even unbeknownst to the college coaches of his school, sometimes made illegal offers and gave illegal gifts to lure prospects to their schools.

The standard joke in recent years among some coaches was that a prominent sports announcer on a national sports show took a cut in pay from what he had received in college. Maybe that was one of the reasons his college received the "Death Penalty" (suspending operation of the entire football program) for numerous recruiting violations.

The recruiting violations were a blot on college football. Although the extent of violations was greatly exaggerated by the media, any cheating was inexcusable. Players receiving money, jewelry, automobiles and summer jobs for which they were not qualified cheapened the game.

An example of stretching the rules was the appointment of an 18-year-old as a vice president of a bank. The bank just happened to be in the state where the prospect chose to attend school. After a year, a neighboring head coach called the president of the bank complaining about the hiring, insinuating that the player was getting paid while not working. The bank president denied the charge and said, in fact, that the vice-president/player had repossessed a few cars of players from the coach's school because of non-payment of loans. Both schools eventually went on NCAA probation.

Suspicions are aroused when a family of limited means suddenly has a $15,000 remodeled kitchen a couple of weeks after their son signs a letter-of-intent.

In the 1960s, a conference that limited a full grant-in-aid scholarship program, allowed for work study. The plum job at one school was, and I am not making this up, to check and see if the stadium was still there.

Today, thanks to the efforts of the American Football Coaches Association and the National Collegiate Athletic Association (NCAA), there are very few serious violations of the rules. In fact, the honesty of football coaches nationwide would fare well in comparison with other segments of society.

The rules today that govern recruiting are sound and give everyone a fighting chance to recruit a prospect. They also take a great deal of pressure off the prospect and his family in making the crucial decision on a college choice.

One fact for sure in recruiting, it is important to sell the parents as well as the prospect. Seldom is a player successfully recruited if mom or dad or both do not approve. I lost a top recruit one time when the mother was for us, and the father was for a West Coast college. The father took the player on an unofficial visit to the competitor's school (perfectly allowable), and the player just happened to have lunch with a famous alumni (who in recent years made headlines for a trip he took down the Southern California freeway in a white Blazer). The player had a very lackluster career, lending credence to the adage, "Some of your best recruits are the ones you lose."

In some cases, girlfriends are another obstacle in the recruiting process. If the relationship is serious, it can be a particular problem; however, mom's preferences normally carry more weight than the sweetheart's in the final decision. One recruit's girlfriend was unusually emphatic in her preference that he stay close to home. During an argument over his college choice, she stabbed him in the rear end with a pair of scissors. Fortunately, his hindquarters were ample enough to ensure his survival, and he made it to Lincoln in relatively good shape.

CHAPTER 17

And Then They're Gone: The Draft

The drafting of athletes from colleges and universities involves some similarities to college recruiting, as well as some differences.

Similarly, they check the character and citizenship of the prospective draftee. They view films and attend games to watch the prospect perform. They speak not only to college coaches, but also to the high school coaches about the prospect's potential to play at a higher level. In some cases, they will fly the college player to visit their coaches and practice facilities.

Some of the differences involve the following:

The professional scouts and/or coaches can physically test the prospect in various drill activities.

They have an extensive rating system to evaluate the draftees, and once they draft a player, he is their property. They don't have to get a letter-of-intent signature.

The professional team has to then deal with the player's agent, many of whom only really care about getting their fee. The college player has four years of actual playing (in a five-year period), whereas the professional player has a contract of various lengths. When the professional player enters some form of free agency, he can shop his talents to the highest bidder. Today, you really do need a "scorecard" to know who is playing for whom.

CLOSING

The intent of this book is not necessarily to teach you EVERYTHING there is to know about football. Rather, it is an attempt to get you a foundation to where you CAN learn all you want to about the sport.

How do you really learn about football? You watch it as though you are a student. That means watching what happens away from the ball as well as watching what happens around the ball. If you see two or three running backs lined up in the backfield before a play, it is more likely a running play than a passing play—but not always. And if you see only one running back, or none (called an empty backfield) it is more likely a passing play than a running play—but not always.

Try and listen to the announcers during the game, especially when they use the "telestratter" to diagram what happened and why it happened on a particular play. And if you are watching a game on television, but the game is being broadcast on the radio, try watching the game with the radio on and the TV sound turned all the way down. The radio announcers, just by the fact they have no images, have to give more detail in describing the play for the listeners.

If you go to a game in person, watch what happens on the sidelines when a defense or offense comes off the field. If you are close enough, you can see what a coach thinks about his team's performance. Often the team will gather in a group, and a coach will draw on a marker board to "make adjustments" to what the other team is doing.

Always pay attention to what is going on between the offensive and defensive line. If the stadium you are at has big-screen TVs to replay each play, watch for key blocks or how someone got open. By understanding why things happen, you will see how and why trends develop during games, giving you a better understanding of the game as well as helping you anticipate what an offense or defense is going to do in a particular situation.

It is also important for someone learning the game—or any student of the game—to watch what teams do differently at the start of the second half. Halftime is about learning what your opponent is doing and adjusting so that you can still be successful. That's why you will hear announcers saying the game was two different stories—the first and second half. One team learned what it needed to do to be successful and did it. The other team, even with an impressive first half, will likely find itself on the short end if it does not adjust at halftime. Sometimes, "adjusting" means making no changes; A team is doing something well and stays with it. Or it finds a weak player on the other team and attacks in the direction of that player time and again for big gains of yards, even scoring. You will hear about how some defensive players—usually defensive backs—are "picked on." Well, they are not picked on because they are stopping the offense. Indeed, the offense goes at them time and time again because they are having success running or passing in the direction of a player the offense has found to be a weak link on the defense. It is a "law of the jungle" mentality, but in the sport of football only the physically and mentally strong survive.

If you have a question and you are a woman who doesn't want to ask your spouse, or if you are a boy or girl who has parents not interested in football, call a local coach or even that coach's radio show. With the negativity that permeates the radio talk shows these days, you would be surprised to find how delighted a coach is to talk about the game itself with a fan. Or call the coach at his office. There is no such thing as a dumb question, especially in football. And you will likely find out that when that one question is answered, it also provides an answer, or a route to the answer, for several other questions you have. Football knowledge is a cumulative thing: a pyramid that needs a lot of blocks for a good foundation, and then fewer, very strategically placed blocks get the fan/student of the game to the top of the knowledge heap.

Most of all, enjoy football. After a while, if you find you just don't enjoy it, then maybe it is just not for you.

On the other hand, if you give yourself a chance, you could find a passion for football and see why many of those around you consider football the best sport of all. There is a sense of the game of RISK to football with the strategic planning and chances that are taken.

Also, football is about being organized and looking ahead, while learning from the past. In many respects, football parallels the game of life. You will often hear about how football players have taken what they have learned in football and applied it to their lives off the field. The work ethic and mental conditioning are things successful business people use every day.

So, maybe you will discover something about yourself as you discover the game of football. While you might have been a novice when you opened this book, you now probably even know a few things that your friends or spouse don't know or don't understand as deeply as you may now understand.

Fill in the blanks where you have questions, and put it all together as you watch your next game. That sounds elementary, yet it is the exact approach we coaches use every week.

You have now graduated *Football 101!*

APPENDIX

REMEMBER, KID... BEFORE YOU INTERVIEW THE LINEBACKERS, ALWAYS TOSS A COUPLE OF LIVE CHICKENS INTO THE ROOM RIGHT BEFORE YOU GO IN...
DEFENSIVE MEETING ROOM
PRESS

FOOTBALL SIGNALS

BALL READY FOR PLAY

START CLOCK

TIMEOUT

TV/RADIO TIMEOUT

TOUCHDOWN, FIELD GOAL POINTS AFTER TOUCHDOWN

SAFETY

BALL DEAD, TOUCHBACK

FIRST DOWN

UNSPORTSMANLIKE CONTACT NONCONTACT FOUL

ILLEGAL PARTICIPATION

SIDELINE INTERFERENCE

RUNNING INTO OR ROUGHING KICKER OR HOLDER

ILLEGAL BATTING ILLEGAL KICKING (followed by pointing toward toe for kicking)

ILLEGAL FAIR CATCH SIGNAL

FORWARD PASS INTERFERENCE KICK-CATCHING INTERFERENCE

ROUGHING PASSER

UNCATCHABLE
FORWARD PASS

OFFSIDE DEFENSE

FALSE START
ENCROACHMENT OFFENSE

ILLEGAL SHIFT (2 hands)
ILLEGAL MOTION (1 hand)

DELAY OF GAME

SUBSTITUTION
INFRACTION

FAILURE TO WEAR
REQUIRED EQUIPMENT

ILLEGAL HELMET
CONTACT

LOSS OF DOWN

INCOMPLETE FORWARD PASS
PENALTY DECLINED
NO PLAY, NO SCORE
TOSS OPTION DELAYED

LEGAL TOUCHING OF
FORWARD PASS OR
SCRIMMAGE KICK

INADVERTENT
WHISTLE

DISREGARD FLAG

END OF PERIOD

SIDELINE WARNING

ILLEGAL TOUCHING
FIRST TOUCHING

ILLEGAL PASS
ILLEGAL FORWARD
HANDING

INTENTIONAL
GROUNDING

INELIGIBLE DOWNFIELD
ON PASS

PERSONAL FOUL

CLIPPING

BLOCKING BELOW WAIST
ILLEGAL BLOCK

CHOP BLOCK

HOLDING/OBSTRUCTING
ILLEGAL USE OF HANDS/ARMS

ILLEGAL BLOCK
IN THE BACK

HELPING RUNNER
INTERLOCKED BLOCKING

TRIPPING

GRASPING FACE MASK
OR HELMET OPENING

PLAYER
DISQUALIFICATION

NEBRASKA'S

Ten Minute Stretching Routine

Note: the shaded area indicates what is being stretched.

1. Pull elbow behind head... Hold easy stretch 10 seconds each arm, 20 seconds total.

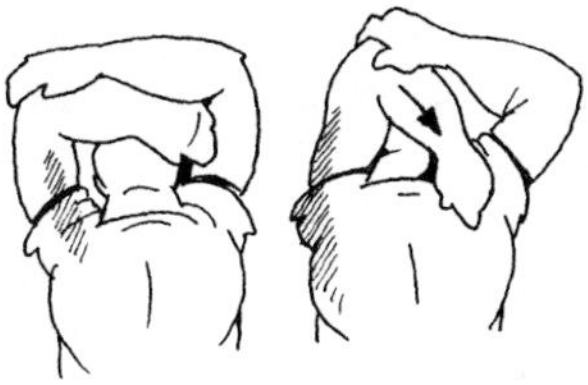

2. Interlace fingers behind your back. Slowly turn your elbows to inside as you keep your arms straight. Your chest should be forward and head straight. 15 Seconds.

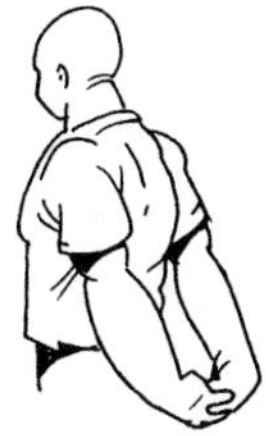

3. With arms extended over head, grab one hand with the other, slowly bend at the waist as you gently pull hand toward floor. Hold an easy stretch 10 seconds each side.

4-A From a standing position with legs straight, slowly bend at waist until you feel an easy stretch in the back of the legs. Do not over-stretch. 30 Seconds.

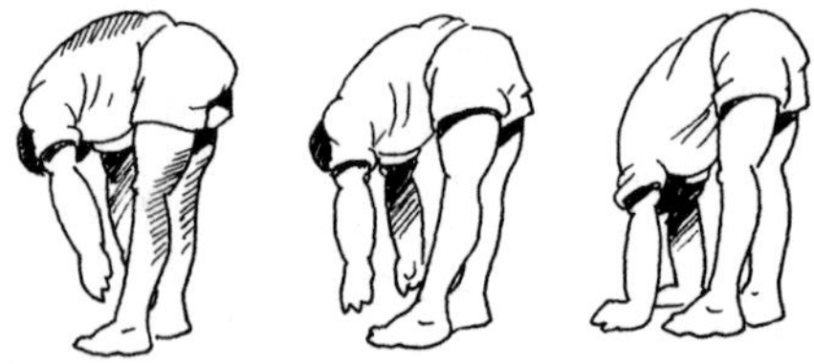

4-B Return to a standing position by slightly bending your knees, and then stand erect. This will take the pressure off the lower back and stretch the hamstrings.

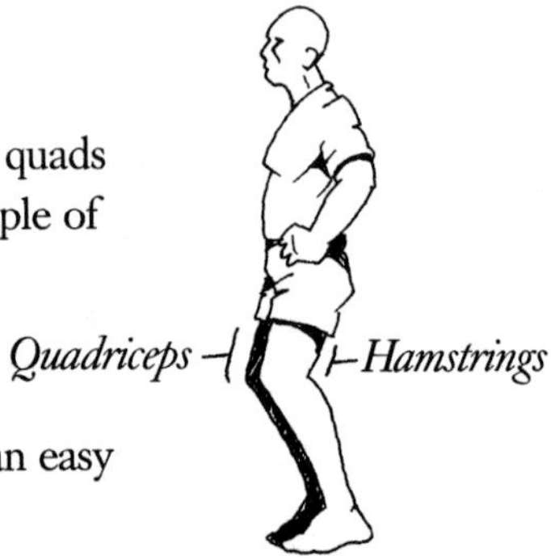

5. 1/4 Squat...Hold 30 seconds. Bring quads into action as hamstrings relax. Principle of reciprocal inhibition.

6. Repeat #4. Hold 25 seconds. Do not bounce when you stretch. Hold an easy stretch. Be relaxed.

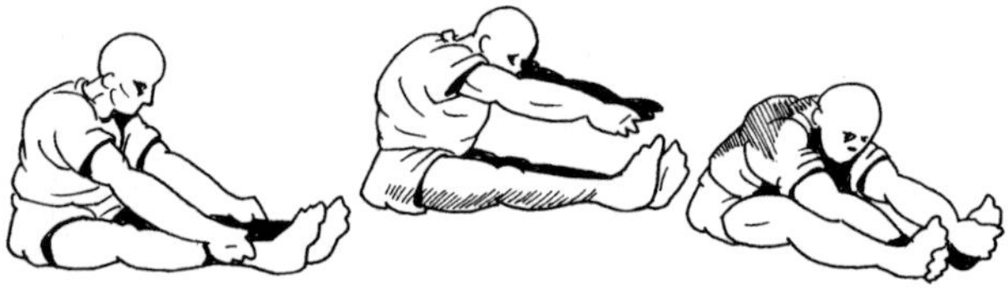

7. Sit down with heels 4 to 8 inches apart. With legs straight slowly bend forward at waist. Hold an easy stretch for 10 seconds. Slightly increase stretch into developmental phase of stretching. Hold for 10 seconds. Use towel if necessary.

10. Pull leg to chest as one unit, one hand around knee and other hand around ankle.

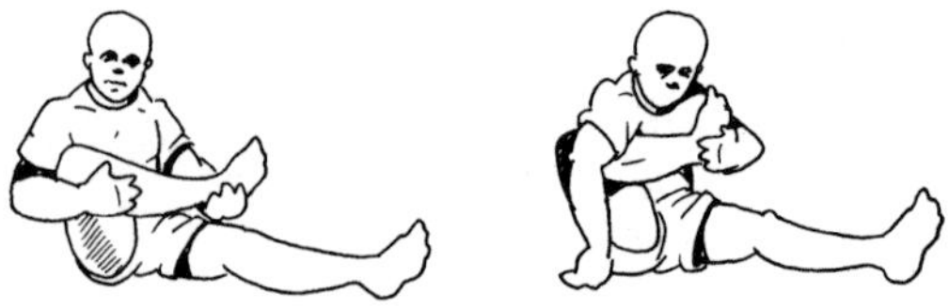

Stretch under control. Do not strain. 20 Seconds.

11. Lay on side, extend lower leg and grab ankle of the top leg. Create stretch in quad. Hold 10 seconds. Makes hurdle stretch easier to do.

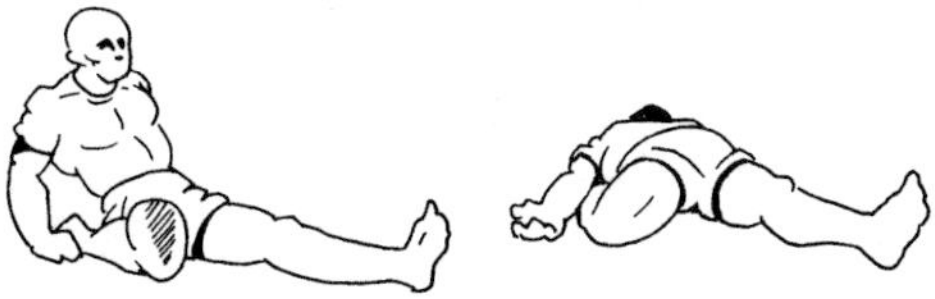

12. Now set the same leg behind you in hurdle stretch. Toe pointed straight back if possible, but do not strain to do it. Slowly lean backwards until you feel the stretch in the quad. Stretch easy and they slowly increase stretch into developmental phase as you relax. 30 Seconds.

13. Then straighten out the bent leg and bring the sole of the other foot to the inside of the other thigh. Now with your foot pointed straight ahead (keep foot relaxed), slowly bend forward at waist to stretch hamstring and back. Hold an easy stretch 5 seconds and developmental 15 seconds. No drastic stretching. 30 Seconds. Use towel if necessary.

14. Repeat exercises 11, 12, 13, 14... Total, 90 seconds.

15. Roll in ball, up and back, 4-6 times. 15 Seconds.

16. Legs over head... Keep knees slightly bent. Use hands on back of hips for support. Hold an easy stretch whenever you can breathe naturally. 20 Seconds.

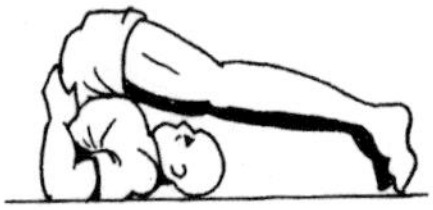

17. From this legs over head position, roll down on spine. Slowly rolling forward...Hitting one vertebrae at a time. Roll slowly and under control 10 seconds. Use hands behind knees or lower legs to help the stretch as you roll. 10 Seconds.

18. Lay flat on back, extend arms over head. Point toes and stretch arms over head as far as you can without a drastic strain. 5 Seconds, then relax.

19. From this lying position, grab one leg just below the knee and pull knee toward chest. Back of head may be up or down. Hold stretch 10 seconds.

20. From #19, pull bent leg over straight leg. If your right leg is bent over use left hand on upper part of thigh to gently pull down as you keep your shoulders flat and extended straight out from the shoulder. This should stretch lower back and side of butt. 20 Seconds. Do not strain.

21. Repeat exercises #19 and #20 with opposite leg. 30 Seconds total.

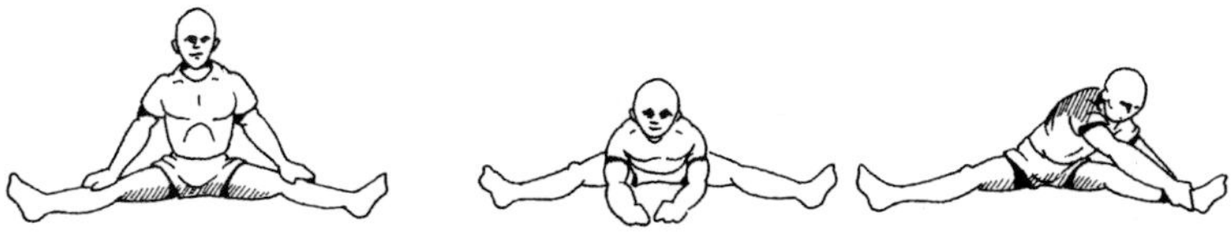

22. A. Sit up with legs straight. Move legs out as far as possible without straining. Keep feet upright and relaxed. Now slowly lean straight forward until you feel strain on inside of legs. Keep hips forward...Hold easy stretch for 20 seconds.

B. Sit up straight. Stretch left hamstring and back by bending at waist toward foot of left leg. Keep head up as you feel a good but controlled stretch of 20 seconds.

C. Other leg. 20 Seconds. Total 60 seconds.

23. Pull soles of feet together, pull forward and hold easy stretch 20 seconds.

24. Saigon squat. 10 Seconds.

25. One leg forward with a bent knee (knee should be directly over ankle). Other leg is directly behind with the knee down. Slowly move hips forward without changing position of front foot or back knee. Hold easy stretch for 15 seconds. Do both sides. 30 Seconds. Should feel stretch in front of hip, hamstring or groin.

DEFINITIONS

SCORING

Touchdown:

While announcers often say that a player has given his team "seven points" when they enter the end zone, a touchdown—running the ball into the end zone, catching a pass in the end zone or running into the end zone after a catch, or recovering a fumble in the end zone—is worth only six points. The touchdown sets up the opportunity for another point via an extra-point kick. The touchdown (TD) also sets up the possibility of two additional points should the team run or pass the ball into the end zone, rather than kicking it for an extra single point from just beyond the two-yard line.

Extra-point kick:

As mentioned, the ball is kicked through the uprights from about 19 yards out after a touchdown.

Two-point conversion:

Rather than try an extra point, teams run or pass the ball into the end zone for two points, making the touchdown worth eight points rather than the conventional seven. Teams use the two-point conversion to make up ground: For example, if a team is trailing 20-12, and they score a touchdown, they are down 20-18, and an extra point leaves them down a point, 20-19. Especially if it is late in the game, a team will go for two points to tie the score at 20-20. Another likely reason to "Go for two" is if a team has missed an extra point kick. Thus, a team up 6-0 scores a touchdown, and is ahead 12-0. They will likely go for two points to make the lead 14-0. Then if the other team scores two TDs and makes two extra points, they will only have tied the score, not going ahead 14-13 (which would be the case if the first team was up 6-0, scored a TD and kicked the extra point for 13 points, rather than the 14 points they get because of the two-point conversion). Also, there are scores in a game where teams will go for two points. If a team scores a touchdown to take a one-point lead, 27-26, they will likely try a two-point conversion. The reason is this: what good does an extra point do? Up 27-26, a field goal by the losing team puts it in the lead. Even kicking in an extra point, 28-26, a field goal by the losing team still puts it in the lead, 29-28. But if the team that scored goes for two points and gets it, they go up by three points, 29-26, meaning a field goal by the other team only ties the score.

Field goal:

Seldom tried from beyond 50-53 yards, a field goal is worth three points if the ball goes through the uprights when it is kicked off the ground. The ball is placed on the ground by the kicker's "holder" about seven yards from the line of scrimmage. Factor in that the goal posts are 10 yards beyond the end zone, and a 50-yard field goal is actually kicked from the 33-yard line (33 plus the seven for the kick, plus the 10 yards for the end zone equals 50). For a right-footed kicker, the misses are either short, hooked to his left or pushed to his right. A bad snap from the center to the holder can mess up the timing between the kicker and the holder, as well as allowing the defensive team a better opportunity to block the kick.

KEY DEFINITIONS/TERMS FOR BEGINNERS

Arm tackle:

This is what happens when players do not use their bodies to make tackles. They try and stop a hard-charging back or receiver by grabbing at him with their arms and hands. Bigger and stronger players are difficult to arm tackle. Arm tackling shows a lack of toughness, effort or technique on a defensive player's part.

Big hole:

At the line of scrimmage, if the offensive line is moving the defenders out of the way, it gives the running back an easy opening to get through. While the running back will gain a lot of yards and be mentioned by the announcers many times, it is the offensive line that should get a lot of the credit. Because there might be a running back on the other team who is faster, stronger or has more ability, yet if that back has nowhere to run, he won't get the impressive numbers, and it will appear he is having a bad day when the reality might be that his offensive line is also having a rough day.

Blown coverage:

When a receiver or back is left all alone and open down the field to catch a pass, it is because a defensive player has forgotten, or lost track of an assignment, and thus the receiver is left alone and open. A blown coverage is dealt with severely because someone, be it a coach or more likely a player, has not fulfilled a responsibility on that play and has let his teammates down, giving the offense a boost in both yardage and momentum.

Broken play:

This occurs when the play that was supposed to be run falls apart because someone did not do what he was supposed to do. These plays usually result in a loss of yards or a turnover.

Downfield blocking:

Good efforts and performances by receivers, and sometimes the linemen, take a short gain into a long gain. If a running back can get past the line of scrimmage (the defensive tackles and perhaps a linebacker or two), then the defense is counting on its defensive backs to make the tackle. If the receivers are blocking the defensive backs and the offensive linemen are doing their job at the line of scrimmage and picking up a linebacker or two down the field a little ways, then the running back finds open field after he gets a few yards past the line of scrimmage.

Field position:

Announcers often refer to this. Field position is simple: it is where a team takes over possession of the ball. If a team has the ball on its own 20-yard-line, or anywhere within those 20 yards closer to its end zone, that is considered "poor" field position. If, however, the team starts from its own 40-yard-line, that is good field position. Starting anywhere in an opponent's territory (from the 50 yard line on in to their end zone) is considered excellent field position. You will hear coaches talking about winning the battle of field position. The team that starts its possessions, or drives, closest to the opponent's end zone has the shortest distance to travel for points—a field goal or touchdown.

Leg whipping:

If an offensive lineman is on the ground, he can't block a player rushing in to sack the quarterback or make a tackle. So in this illegal maneuver, the lineman swings his legs up and hits the defender around the knees. In addition to being a penalty, leg whipping drives defenders to extreme anger because the knee injuries it can produce may end a defender's career.

Looking off (a receiver):

The best quarterbacks are the ones who throw the ball where the defense is not expecting it. That is, if a quarterback has a receiver in mind, the defense will know it if it sees the quarterback staring at that receiver from the time the ball is snapped. Thus, the quarterback has to be able to give the defense the impression he is throwing the ball to someone else. At the last instant he turns and throws the ball to the intended receiver. The more experienced the quarterback, usually the better he "looks off" his receivers. Many interceptions occur because the defense sees the quarterback eyeing the same receiver an entire play, allowing the defense to anticipate where the pass is going.

Motion:

To re-position a player or to read and/or confuse the defense, receivers, running backs and tight end are sent "in motion" before a play by the quarterback while the rest of the team is lined up at the line of scrimmage. Only one player can move at a time, and a player lined up at or near the line or scrimmage can only move laterally—he can neither move forward before the snap, nor fake the appearance of going forward in an attempt to draw the defense offsides. (A running back can move toward the line of scrimmage before he begins a lateral motion as he gets within a yard or two of the line of scrimmage.)

Onsides kick:

When a team is trailing and there is not much time left, instead of kicking the ball deep on kickoffs, they will kick the ball short and try to recover it. On all kickoffs, the ball must travel at least 10 yards before the ball is considered "Live" and the kicking team can recover it. The kicker usually kicks the ball on the ground to the side where he has almost all of his players lined up. The receiving team, usually aware that an onside kick is coming, puts players used to handling the ball (receivers, tight ends, running backs and defensive backs) 10 yards from where the ball is kicked off, thus increasing their chances of having a "sure-handed" player catch the ball as the kicking team is seeking to regain the ball.

Open-field tackle:

This happens when a back or receiver has a lot of open field in which to run and only one player stands in the way. Should the defensive player not tackle the back in the open field, the play will go for a big gain, or a touchdown. Usually, watching on TV, you will see only one defender in the frame when the announcer talks about a great "open-field tackle."

Quick kick:

Facing third down and "long" (a distance that will likely not be achieved on the third down play), the offensive team, instead of waiting for fourth down, punts the ball on third down. The goal is to catch the defense off-guard, so the punt will roll as far as possible, and since the defense is not expecting a punt, there will be no return. The quick kick occurs much less frequently these days, but is still occasionally deployed.

Sack:

A sack occurs when the defense tackles the quarterback for a loss of yards as the quarterback tries to pass the ball. If a team "blitzes" (sends more than just the defensive linemen, including linebackers and/or defensive backs), it puts more pressure on the quarterback, but it also leaves fewer defenders up the field to cover the offense's receivers. Some sacks are referred to as "coverage sacks" because the quarterback has enough time to throw, but can't find an open receiver. The quarterback is thus sacked because he has nowhere to throw the ball because he holds it too long. Defenders are also credited for "hurried passes" (making the quarterback throw the ball before he is really ready to, but has to because of a lot of pressure from the defense) and "knockdowns" (legally hitting the quarterback as he is in the motion of throwing, but not being credited with a "sack" of the quarterback because the ball has been thrown. Knockdowns take the same sort of physical toll as a sack—ask any quarterback).

Slant route:

You will hear this play occasionally when a receiver is injured. The receiver runs from the spot he is lined up at near the sideline toward the center of the field. This places him in the heart of the opposing team's defense. Yet, because he is running diagonally across the field, he is often open, despite the fact that there are several defenders in the area. While the pattern is highly successful in making completions, it is also highly likely that the receiver, once he catches the ball, is going to encounter a defender, one he did not see because he was running diagonally. These hits often make the highlight film, but they are a lowlight to the receiver. The hits are so hard that often the defensive player gets up as slowly as the receiver simply because of the violent collision.

Squib kick:

Done on a kickoff, the kicker hits the ball on a wobbly, low sort of kick, rather the high, towering kicks usually seen on kickoffs. It is done to prevent the return team's speedy deep return players (lined up at the goal line) from returning the ball. Thus, a non-speed player is the target of a squib kick. This is usually used late in a half as time is winding down, and the kicking team seeks to prevent a big return, especially one for a touchdown.

Shanked punt:

A punter hits the ball off the side of his foot. While punts usually cover about 40 yards, shanked punts go a fraction of that. It usually results in good field position for the receiving team while resulting in a lecture to the punter (and maybe even a spot on the bench as someone else takes over the punting duties) from the kicking team's coach.

Trenches:

This term is also referred to as "in the trenches" or the "battle of the trenches" The trenches are the line of scrimmage or the point where the ball is snapped on each play. Thus, the battle in the trenches is conducted between the offensive line and defensive line for each team. If the offensive team has a lot of yards and/or points, it is winning the battle of the trenches. That is, its offensive line is pushing the defensive line back up the field or out of the way, so its running backs can run and its quarterback has time to pass. If a team has few yards or points, then the defensive line is winning the battle of the trenches, the offensive linemen pushing backward or away and tackling the quarterback and running backs before the offensive team can gain many yards. Coaches call this, as well as the turnover ratio, the key to winning—or losing—games.

Stiff arm:

Usually done by running backs but sometimes by receivers after they catch the ball. It involves a back putting his arm and hand out (the one not holding the ball), usually toward the upper body or facemask of a defensive player pursuing him, and pushing the defender away. The move is just enough to knock a pursuing player out of step or off line when done correctly. It is an attempt to push a defender away, or separate the defender from the player he is closing in on.

Two-minute drill:

When there are two minutes left in the first or second half, teams develop an urgency to score because time is running out. The offensive team will run its two-minute drill, trying to stop the clock by getting out of bounds after catching a pass or running the ball. Often two plays are called in the huddle or all plays are called without a huddle. The QB may also spike the ball at his feet to stop the clock. The two-minute drill produces a lot of excitement because there is nothing lackadaisical on either side of the ball.

Turnovers:

Teams live and die (win and lose) by how they "take care of the ball," which means whether they fumble it or have it intercepted. The "turnover ratio" shows how well a team takes care of the ball and how opportunistic it is in taking the ball from the other team. Thus, if you get four fumbles and two interceptions from a team, and only fumble the ball away to them one time yourself, you have a turnover rating of plus-five, which is extremely good. Teams with high plus numbers in turnovers win more often than not. The worst teams in the league almost always have the highest negative number when it comes to turnover ratio. Too many fumbles will cause a running back to be pulled from a game or even released or traded from a team. Along the same lines, a quarterback who throws a lot of interceptions will find himself on the bench or out of work.

"Tweener":

A player who is "between" sizes; for example, a defensive lineman usually weighs at least 280 pounds whereas a linebacker weighs 230-250 pounds. So a player who weighs 260-265 pounds would be a "tweener" between linebacker and lineman. That is, he is too small to be a true defensive lineman, but too big (especially if he does not have good speed) to be a linebacker. So he either has to put on weight, lose weight or increase his speed.

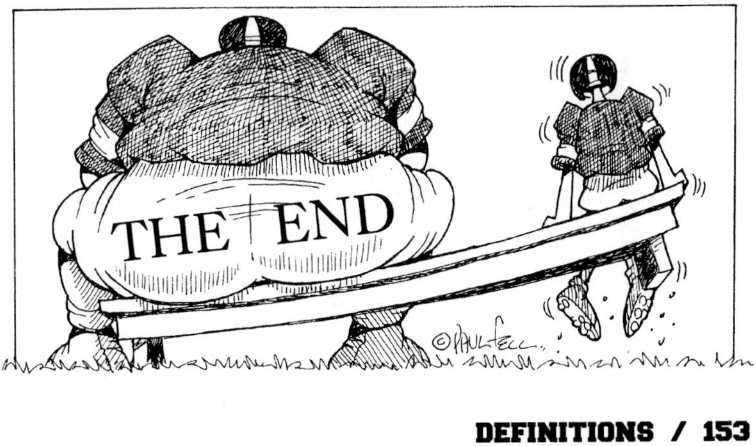